THE PASTOR

D1362319

"Lathrop connects the dots between the Gospel lived in the Sunday gathering and the vocational and spiritual lives of pastors—and all others in search of a deeper life of faith and action. The spirituality of which this book speaks and the pastoral vocation it redefines are both biblical and Christological symbols, and at the same time profoundly in-fleshed theological realities. The words at the heart of this rich and reorienting book take their life from, and speak to, the very real things we encounter as the people of God gather for its liturgical life: the assembly itself, baptism, the Word, the prayers, the Table Meal, all these things, for the pastor and for the people, forming an outward-bound spirituality for the sake of a needy world. This is a volume to have, to hold, and to mark, as it is said of all good things."

Gláucia Vasconcelos Wilkey
School of Theology and Ministry
Seattle University

CONTENTS

DEDICATION

for Miriam Schmidt

*and for Mark Mummert, Dirk Lange,
Melinda Quivik, and John Saraka*

with gratitude and love

PREFACE

This book is intended as an ecumenical reflection on the identity and central tasks of the ordained leader who lives and works in relationship with a current, public Christian assembly. That leader—called by this book "the pastor"—might also, in that community, be called by another name: "priest" or "elder," "minister" or "preacher," or even sometimes "father" or "mother" or "reverend." Whatever the name used, however, the book is meant as a sign of encouragement for such a leader and an invitation to deeper engagement with those central tasks of the office, to deeper heart for the pastoral undertaking in a difficult time. It is meant as the outline of a particular spirituality, rooted in baptism and the liturgy, a spirituality that might be a lively, graceful, engaged, and humble way for pastors to be and to walk in the world.

The title is simple because I hope that the book will be found to be relatively simple. Of course, I long for it to be a book of wisdom, of the serpent-kind, as well as a book of straightforwardness and humility, of the dove-kind. But mostly I long for it to be an homage of respect, a profound bow, to faithful pastors and to those who struggle to know what faithfulness may be in such a time as this. I hope for it to be a drink of cool water on a hot day, a shelter and beginning place for thought, and a moment of deliberate delight in the central matters of Christian ministry. In spite of all the struggles, one psalm that the Christian community anciently gave its clergy to read as of themselves sang out, "The boundary lines have fallen for me in pleasant places; I have a goodly heritage" (Ps. 16:6). I hope this book may explore those boundary lines. And I hope it may welcome into its pages the current ordained leadership of many churches, as well as seminary students and any others who want to think about the pastoral vocation.

But the book is not a law book. It is not the final description of a single model for the clergy. It is certainly not intended as a judgment on anyone. Paul's wisdom still applies, even against our own self-accusations, let alone against this book were it to function in judgment. Let the pastors say,

> Think of us in this way, as servants of Christ and stewards of God's mysteries. Moreover, it is required of stewards that they be found trustworthy. But with me it is a very small thing that I should be judged by you or by any human court. I do not even judge myself....but I am not thereby acquitted. It is the Lord who judges me. (1 Cor. 4:1-4)

To say this is not to let us off the hook. It is required of the stewards of God's mysteries that they be trustworthy. The intention here may indeed sometimes be that we call each other to such trustworthiness. But it is God who judges justly. The task of this book cannot be that judgment.

No, this book is rather a venture, a proposal, a question, the reflections of one pastor after thirty-seven years of ordained ministry. That is why, throughout the text, you will find instances and images from my own experience—instances of my own use of the first-person singular pronoun—set off in italics and set in counterpoint to the main body of the text. You may choose to skip these passages, but you do need to know that this is the person who is writing this book. Furthermore, the book is the work of a *Lutheran* pastor, one who has promised to do his public work in the context of commitment to a given communal confession. It follows—as belongs to this confession—that the focus here will be upon the "ministry of Word and Sacrament" and upon the texts of the "catechism." But, since these very things may be regarded as the baptismal heritage of all Christians, and since they function at the center of many Christian communities, perhaps the author's Lutheran commitment may serve the book's ecumenical purpose. Finally, the book is the work of a liturgist. It should be no wonder, then, that the text seeks to call pastors to find the center of their vocational identity, the heart of their spirituality, in the communal tasks of presiding at the holy table and at the holy bath, of preaching, and of seeing to it that there is a collection to be justly distributed among the poor. Herein lies the venture of the book, its question, its proposal: if it is for the sake of these communal actions that we ordain people at all, cannot these things be taken as the center and focus for pastoral identity and pastoral spirituality? What might such a spirituality be like?

The book begins by seeking to define the terms *pastor* and *spirituality* and to set out both the baptismal catechism and the central pastoral-liturgical tasks as the framework for further reflection (the introduction). Then, a spirituality for the pastor is proposed in which these central tasks are learned by heart (part 1), and life itself, also for the pastor, is drawn as a gift from the matters that live at the heart of the assembly (part 2).

This book is consciously dependent upon earlier works, most especially the remarkable *Country Parson* by the seventeenth-century Anglican pastor and poet, George Herbert. One might simply read Herbert and be done with it. His book is quite enough. In fact, even the chapter titles here may recall his own: "The Parson Preaching," "The Parson in Sacraments," "The Parson's Courtesy," and "The Parson's Knowledge," for example. Several of Herbert's sayings may recur here, too, at least in hidden ways. For example, this:

> The character of his Sermon is Holiness...gained first, by choosing texts of Devotion, not Controversy, moving and ravishing texts, whereof the Scriptures are full. Secondly, by dipping and seasoning all our words and sentences in our hearts, before they come into our mouths, truly affecting and cordially expressing all that we say; so that the auditors may plainly perceive that every word is heart-deep. (*The Parson Preaching*)

And this:

> Neither will they believe him in the pulpit whom they cannot trust in his Conversation. (*The Parson's Life*)

And this:

> Especially at Communion times he is in a great confusion, as being not only to receive God, but to break, and administer him. Neither finds he any issue in this, but to throw himself down at the throne of grace...(*The Parson in Sacraments*)

And this:

> So, if any neighboring village be overburdened with poor, and his own less charged, he finds some way of relieving it...representing to his people, that the Blessing of God to them ought to make them the more charitable, and not the less...(*The Parson in Reference*)

And this:

> The country Parson is generally sad, because he knows nothing but the Cross of Christ...or if he have any leisure to look off from thence, he meets continually with two most sad spectacles, Sin and Misery....Nevertheless, he sometimes refresheth himself, as knowing that nature will not bear everlasting droopings....Wherefore he condescends to human frailties both in himself and others; and intermingles some mirth in his discourses...(*The Parson in Mirth*)

And, finally, this:

> The Country Parson is a Lover of old Customs, if they be good, and harmless...(*The Parson's Condescending*)

But such texts are not easy to read. They can readily be taken as judgment and absolute law. They require constant recontextualization and reinterpretation—not least, in that steady use of the masculine pronoun, both for the pastor and for God—such that their distance from us easily overwhelms their beauty or their usefulness or delight. We might still understand *preaching* and *sacraments* and *the parson's life*, but then we would probably need to read "social action" instead of *reference*, "sense of humor" instead of *mirth*, and, notably, "interest in cultural practices" or "delight in the good things of the world" instead of *condescending*.

Do read Herbert, especially if you are skilled at rereading and, perhaps more, at deconstructing and rewriting. But here we need to try to say something like his counsel again, now, at this moment, for today's pastors. Still, we need to speak with humility, above all not saying too much, and always knowing that we nonetheless keep company with many, many pastors through the ages who have also tried to articulate the vocation: Augustine and John Chrysostom and Gregory the Great and—shall we not say the truth?—Julian of Norwich and Hildegard of Bingen, as well as Martin Luther and George Herbert and Richard Baxter and Urban Holmes and, now, even the realistic though fictional preacher of Marilynne Robinson, in her stunning novel *Gilead*.

Among these, here is one venture, one proposal. Call it simply *The Pastor*. And subtitle it *A Spirituality*. I hope it may be helpful for you.

Gordon W. Lathrop
Eastertide 2006
Commemoration of Julian of Norwich

The Pastor's Lifelong Catechumenate

The pastor lives among symbols. The pastor cares for symbols, sets out symbols for other people, hopes these symbols may hold people's lives into meaning. Symbols are, as Gerard Manley Hopkins would say, the "gear and tackle and trim" of pastoral ministry. Or they ought to be. Words, stories, sacraments, images, gestures: pastors have really nothing else. No wonder, then, that the pastor can take on the character of these surroundings, these materials and tools of the work. No wonder that she or he can become—to many other people, often to society and certainly to the community of his or her service—also a symbol. A beginning place for our reflections here on spirituality can be found in this idea—*the pastor among symbols, as a symbol*. Whatever a spirituality for pastors may turn out to be, it will surely include the lifelong relearning of the symbols with which pastors deal and also, along with that relearning, the lifelong venture—and danger—of living as a symbol.

THE PASTOR, AMONG SYMBOLS, AS A SYMBOL

There may be a clerical collar around the pastor's neck. There may be a cross or an icon on the wall of the pastor's study. But the world of symbols that pastors inhabit needs to run deeper than clothing, wider than wall images, though these things may matter as secondary reflections of that world. Rather, the primary symbols in a Christian pastor's care ought to be several quite specific things, basically communal in their practice, historic in their ecumenical centrality, widely resonant in their meaning. Christians have believed that these things, summarized in the

1

phrase "Word and sacraments," are the gift of God and the heart of any faithful ministry. Indeed, such ministry is sometimes called "the ministry of Word and Sacrament."

Already in the second century of this era, Justin's description of the Sunday meeting of Christians in the city of Rome gave us an outline of the ordained leader's tasks. For Justin, the "presider" preaches a biblical sermon, gives thanks at the table as well as possible, and sees to it that there is a collection for the poor. The text (*1 Apology 67*) is worth quoting again, accenting these classic tasks of the leader:

> And for the rest after these things [after baptism is enacted] we continually remind each other of these things [of baptism]. Those who have the means help all those who are in want, and we continually meet together. And over all that we take to eat we bless the creator of all things through God's Son Jesus Christ and through the Holy Spirit. And on the day named after the sun all, whether they live in the city or the countryside, are gathered together in unity. Then the records of the apostles or the writings of the prophets are read for as long as there is time. When the reader has concluded, *the presider in a discourse admonishes and invites us into the pattern of these good things.* Then we all stand together and offer prayer. And, as we said before, when we have concluded the prayer, bread is set out to eat, together with wine and water. *The presider likewise offers up prayer and thanksgiving, as much as he can,* and the people sing out their assent saying the *amen.* There is a distribution of the things over which thanks have been said and each person participates, and these things are sent by the deacons to those who are not present. Those who are prosperous and who desire to do so, give what they wish, according to each one's own choice, and *the collection is deposited with the presider. He aids orphans and widows, those who are in want through disease or through another cause, those who are in prison, and foreigners who are sojourning here. In short, the presider is a guardian to all those who are in need.* We all hold this meeting together on the day of the sun since it is the first day, on which day God, having transformed darkness and matter, made the world. On the same day Jesus Christ our savior rose from the dead…he appeared to his apostles and disciples

and taught them these things which we have presented also to you for your consideration.

We still recognize this role. For us, it might be said in this way: Pastors interpret the words and stories of the Bible, holding them out as symbols around which a community may gather, through which members of that community may newly understand the world and their own lives. Furthermore, pastors preside at that important symbolic meal we call by different names—the Holy Communion, the Lord's Supper, the Eucharist, the Mass—holding out loaf and cup as signs and symbols of the death and life of Christ, of the mercy of God, of the Spirit-united community. Pastors preside in the midst of that process whereby children and adults are washed with the great symbolic washing called Baptism and thereby are joined to the assembly that gathers around the symbols of the Bible and the table. Pastors preside in the midst of that assembly—"church," we call it—itself a powerful symbol. They care about a collection of gifts in that assembly, intended for mission and for the relief of the needy, symbols of the mission of God. Finally, pastors carry extensions of these same central symbols into places that need them: words from the Bible and prayers formed by the promises of the Bible; the bread and cup of the meal; food or money from the collection; signs from the bath—words again, words of forgiveness, for example, and perhaps also oil for anointing; and also *people*—the pastors themselves and sometimes others too, as representatives of the assembly, of the church. Many of these may be brought to bedsides of the sick, hospices for the dying, kitchens for the homeless, social-service institutions, refugee camps, prisons, battlefields, places of need. These same things are carried personally into the lives and hearts of the fearful, the guilty, the uncomforted, the confused, but also into wedding parties, new homes, places of new beginnings. The pastor lives with symbols.

The collar around his or her neck—for all of its origin at a time when it indicated that the clergyman belonged to the upper class, to the *gentlemen*, the educated, even the courtiers—may now function usefully and in a different way than that class-based origin. Used carefully, it may help the pastor take on this communal role as bearer of symbols, just as it may also help those around her or him to welcome that role. The icon or cross on the wall, marking a space where the symbols are being made pastorally available to individual need or where the communal use of the symbols is being planned, can invite the pastor and others to an encounter with the deepest intention of such symbolic practice. Something similar can be said of yet other secondary symbols—holy books and vestments, concrete and visible practices of prayer, candles, more icons, even shelves full of volumes representing learned study—none of which are central; none of which are required for being a pastor; all of which may be tangibly helpful.

The pastor lives with symbols.

In a society often starved for meaningful symbolic practice, this pastor may then discover that she or he is the only keeper of communal symbols in sight. Many people may turn to the pastor for a few appropriate words in a time of need or change, for a shared ritual on an occasion of loss, or for counsel on a rite of human passage when—as at a wedding or a birth or a death—the group discovers it has lost whatever rites it once had and does not know where to begin. Sometimes, on such an occasion, just the *presence* of the pastor may seem enough: the pastor then is the symbol—for mystery, for wider connection, for a barely remembered past, perhaps for good, most likely for God. If a symbol is *a gathering place for communal encounter with larger meaning* or *a thing that enables participation in that to which it refers*, then the pastor may indeed be a symbol. One way or another, the pastor learns to live as a symbol.

But if you are a pastor, you know that you need to be careful at this point. The symbols that live at the heart of Christian life are a specific sort of symbol. The sacred words of the Scripture, their collection together into a significant book, and the practice of their holy reading in an assembly might suggest that here we will receive glorious, shimmering, world-making myths, the deeds of mighty figures, words that take us out of this world simply in the hearing. But, in fact, these are stories and poems of ordinary and needy people, of sin and death and loss and hope in this world, and of the passion and anger and surprising mercy of God in dealing with these people. They are words that have room for us, in this world. Such is the Christian holy book. Furthermore, the meal that we keep, in its intensity and focus, its staple food and festive drink, its ceremonial welcome of a wide circle, might suggest that we are consuming magical food, food of the angels, a heavenly banquet, food that will grant us immortality. Then we hear the content of the feast: "the body of Christ, the blood of Christ, given for you." A specific, real death is proclaimed, and if "immortality" is given, then this is a new kind of freedom from death, coming in a world-affirming, bounded, palpable, and mortal way, *here*. More: this holy assembly enlivened by the Holy Spirit is a gathering of the needy and the sinful.

This saving bath that joins us to the holy assembly is an act that identifies us with the crucified Jesus Christ and so with all those with whom he identifies: the little, neglected, oppressed, poor, dying, sinful, marginal ones of the world. These symbols enable participation in the wonderful things to which they refer only by taking us to a place we had not expected, gathering us around a thing we thought far away from meaning and hope, inviting us to faith. They are all *broken symbols*—powerful still in their reference, in the hope they evoke, but made up of the unexpected, the ordinary, the failed, the equivocal rather than the absolute—made up of the *cross*. These broken symbols gather us—our deepest hopes, our very selves—into the circles of their reference, but then they lead us not to possession or control but to *faith*.

Just so, if the pastor is a symbol, that symbol needs to be understood as broken.

Pastors have experience in being expected to be like *shamans*. Most human societies of both history and prehistory have known the work of these adepts of religious connection, these specialists renowned for both their demonstrations of power and their communally convincing tricks. Shamans are the ancient and powerful religious leaders who have been regarded as able to make liaison between the living community and the surrounding spirits or between the living community and its dead. Pastors sometimes seem to be expected to do the same. Or, to say it another way, pastors have lived with being regarded as symbols, as both pointers toward the divine and ways that people can actually participate in mystery, hope, and God. Like shamans, pastors can be seen as able to talk to God for us, able to speak wisdom from the spirits to us, able to get our dead to the right place, perhaps even able to get us all out of here to someplace safe. Again, a responsible pastor will want to be careful here. Unbroken, these expectations can lead to massive disappointment for the community, an impossible burden for the pastor, and huge distortions of Christian meaning for us all. The tragic stories of clergy burnout, clergy abuse, and tyrannical clericalism document this disappointment and distortion.

The pastor must be a broken symbol. If this person is a Christian pastor, the God to whom she or he refers must be the Christian God. Faith trusts that this God gives life where life cannot be, makes something out of nothing, justifies the ungodly, uses the good things of the earth to pour out mercy and bring us again and again to faith, and makes a band of ordinary and needy people into bearers of the Spirit and witnesses to this mercy. Of course the pastor will be a symbol, evoking all that we ever hope to find in a religious leader and a holy connection-maker. We need such a symbol among us, and we would be fooling ourselves if we thought we could live without it. A responsible steward of the mysteries awakens among us the hope for Mystery. Such a steward will carry that role with intention and dignity. But the content of the pastor's work, like the content of the Bible, the Eucharist, and Baptism themselves, must continually surprise these expectations, turning our religious hopes toward new references: the community gathered around the mercy of God in ordinary life; the community gathered around the life-giving cross; the community brought to new maturity in finding such mercy and life here, within our daily limits; the community open to the stranger and to a wider world in need of mercy and life; and that very mercy and life also given to the beggar-among-beggars who is the pastor.

A pastor lives with symbols, is a symbol. But a profound spirituality for pastors must involve a lifelong engagement with the reversals and surprises of these symbols.

Broken Titles

Think of some of the common English titles for this Christian office of leadership: priest, presbyter, elder, preacher, minister, reverend, rector, pastor. Taken in a certain way, these are all good names, if never quite fully accurate to the content of the job. But both their inaccuracy and their diversity make it clear how difficult it is to delineate this office and explain its meaning apart from reference to something else. That "something else" must finally be the assembly for which this leader is appointed and the Word that lives in the heart of that assembly. The ordained one does not make religious connections alone, like a powerful shaman, but only in the midst of the assembly and in relationship to that Word. We would have no pastors without these assemblies. We would have no Christian assemblies without this Word. The pastor must be continually becoming transparent to the very Word and sacraments in the midst of the assembly, the very things for which she or he was appointed in the first place.

So, a *priest* is literally a figure who offers sacrifices. A priest leads the animals up to an altar and cuts their throats. A priest leads the victim to the top of the mountain or the top of the pyramid. Or a priest sets out meat or blood or bread or perhaps merely flowers to try to persuade the deity to give something good back to the offerers in return. But Christian leaders offer no sacrifices—or they ought not. Here is one basic religious surprise of the Christian faith: the God known in that faith does not need or require gifts of any kind. The very idea is repugnant to the denunciations of the Hebrew prophets, to the song of the most profound Hebrew psalms, and to what we can know of the teaching of Jesus: "Go and learn what this means, 'I desire mercy, not sacrifice'" (Matt. 9:13; cf. 12:7). Then why do some Christians call the presiders in their assemblies priests? Perhaps it is because the songs and prayers of the assembly, the songs and prayers that accompany the practice of reading the Bible and celebrating the meal, can be called metaphorically "a sacrifice of praise." The "priest," then, presides in the midst of this singing and praying, helping it to happen communally. Perhaps the gifts gathered in a Christian assembly and intended for the relief of our neighbors' need can be called metaphorically "offerings," and the pastor-priest presides in the midst of this collection, making sure that it takes place and that the gifts are responsibly distributed where they are needed. Or perhaps it is because in preaching and at the table—called metaphorically an "altar"—this presider proclaims the death of Christ, that event regarded by Christians as ending all sacrifice once and for all. In any case, this name for the presider is a *metaphor*, the wrong word used intentionally. The name comes to its purpose, makes its astonishing point, only when it is broken, only when it is not taken literally, and only when it is situated where it belongs—in the assembly. A pastor is not a "priest" alone. A pastor is only a priest metaphorically, in the assembly and in the extensions of the assembly to places of need, as a broken symbol. The assembly itself, called and formed by the Spirit, has the vocation to be together a community of priests for the sake of the world. Used only of the presider and taken literally, the title will mislead us. Allowed to function as a broken symbol, the title can be yet another invitation to the freeing surprises of Christian faith.

But go on. *Presbyter* is the Greek word for *elder*, and some Christian communities apply both words to their ordained leaders. In fact, the English word *priest* (as also *prêtre* in French, *Priester* in German, and *prest* in the Scandinavian languages), known to us as the word used to translate many words in other languages that mean "one who sacrifices," was originally simply a version of *presbyter*. The older idea, older than the idea of sacrifice that came to be so widespread in medieval Christianity, was that a presider was always a person of grey hair.

Priest originally meant *elder*, being a contraction of *presbyter*. In any case, elders, by this expectation, are always wise, insightful, capable of contacting divinity simply because of the dignity of their old age, and therefore are they Christian leaders. But this expectation is simply not true. Some older people are indeed wise, but many of us know also old fools. Age is no guarantee of either insight or holiness, and young people have often been the leaders of Christian assemblies. "Let no one despise your youth," say the pastoral epistles (1 Tim. 4:12), probably paradigmatically. Then why did most ancient Christian assemblies and many modern ones call their leaders elders or presbyters? Perhaps because the wisdom we long for from elders is finally—also for elders themselves—the wisdom of the Spirit in the Bible, in the life-giving meal, in the bath. In these is the old, wise, world-holding story. Then grey hairs are taken on metaphorically (cf. Wis. 4:9) by anyone who faithfully, transparently takes up the leadership of a meeting that is focused around these things. More: the crucified Christ is the wisdom of God, and he is the content of Word, table, and bath. Regardless of age, the presider in such a meeting may be called "elder" metaphorically, as a broken symbol. The actual wisdom is found neither in his or her youth, nor in his or her age, neither in innocent earnestness nor measured gravity—though these things may help us, give us symbolic materials for the breaking—but in the Crucified One given away for the life of the world.

And go on. "The *reverend*," some people say of their pastor. The word, belonging more usually to written language and to lists or mailing addresses, is used also orally in colloquial speech. It paints the person of whom it is used as a person to be revered, as holy, good, sacred. But the New Testament has even Jesus saying, "Why do you call me good? No one is good but God alone" (Mark 10:18). And while some Christians call their male ordained leaders "*father*," Matthew's Gospel has a similar prohibition: "Call no one your father on earth, for you have one Father—the one in heaven" (23:9). Of course we will use these titles—and, perhaps increasingly, "*mother*," as well—but we will need to know that they are the wrong words. They can be true only as broken symbols, as metaphors. It is God the Rock, sending the Spirit, alive in the word of the cross, given away in the central matters of the meeting, who gives us birth and is the only Holy One. Perhaps these words can be used of the community's leader because she or he presides in the midst of that meeting. But we have to say that these particular words are much more difficult to so break, much harder to take other than literally.

It is as if, in their use, we create a little, local patriarchy—or, more uncommonly, a matriarchy. Or it is as if we make the church our family, and we want to cling closely to that family, without examining its dynamics. We need to note that the family image for the community of Jesus in the Gospels has multiple brothers and sisters, mothers and children, but no fathers (Mark 10:30), as if to reject explicitly a community marked by father rule. In the Christian community we should probably do without "father" and "mother" and "reverend"—and certainly "most reverend" or "holy father"—altogether.

Something similar might be said of *rector*. The word means "ruler." But then we stumble against that word of Jesus: "You know that among the Gentiles those whom they recognize as their rulers lord it over them, and their great ones are tyrants over them. But it is not so among you" (Mark 10:42-43a). *Rule*, then, must become a metaphor for its very opposite—service. "Whoever wishes to become great among you must be your servant" (10:43b). Even more, the rector may indeed rule by serving an assembly gathered around the central things, but it is the One present at the heart of those things—the Crucified One giving himself away, washing feet, sharing the lot of the least—who is the Servant, to whom the symbol finally points. Jesus Christ is "ruler" from the cross. Shall it be better for us, then, to use *minister*, the Latin-formed English word that translates the Greek *diakonos* and means "servant"? Perhaps. Except that the original connotation is almost gone from its common meaning. "Minister" is, after all, also the title of high government officials, including the prime minister of various countries in the news. And even in churches, "minister" still trails along its connotations of position, power, and high respect. "Minister," too, only works if one constantly translates it and constantly refers to the things and people this server is serving. Even then, "serving" can be its own way of garnering personal power, gathering others around my serving self, standing in for the Lord Jesus, and creating dependencies. In the church, the serving needs to be mutual and freeing and always in witness to the one called the Servant. Serving comes as a gift of the Spirit to the entire community.

Yet the rector, the minister, Fr. John Smith, the Rev. Jane Doe themselves are indeed worthy of respect. Or, rather, their very presence and existence evokes our hope for profound and holy leadership. Their very presence is a symbol. How shall it be a broken symbol? And how shall they then live with being such a symbol? These are questions these somewhat problematic but very real titles raise. But they are also questions that live at the heart of a healthy spirituality for clergy.

Preacher and *presider* might seem more like it. They seem to be functional words, describing what an ordained leader does in the meeting. But even they are complex. Commonly, people take it that "preachers" simply "preach"—that is, they authoritatively tell other people what to do, often in ways that are not pleasant. It begins to sound again like "lording it over them." But the New Testament has a different conception. Preaching is certainly telling the truth about our need and sin, a thing that often is not pleasant. But at root Christian preaching is supposed to be the announcement of good news. More profoundly, for Paul, for example, preaching is speaking about the cross of Jesus and its life-giving meaning in the midst of the assembly: "I did not come proclaiming the mystery of God to you in lofty words or wisdom. For I decided to know nothing among you except Jesus Christ, and him crucified" (1 Cor. 2:1b-2). Or, for Luke, preaching involves Jesus himself, in the power of the Spirit, bringing good news to the poor and release to the captives (Luke 4:18), and opening hearts and minds to understand the Scriptures (Luke 24:32, 45). For Luke, these things continue to take place in the assembly. And "presiding" also needs to be held in context. It, too, must not be directing any kind of ritual, with the massive authority of a "president," but presiding in service and love at bath, Word, and table, in the midst of a participating assembly. Both presiding and preaching need to be reinterpreted—exercised with authority, but broken to Christian purpose.

All of these titles for an ordained leader in a Christian assembly can be made to work. None of them is quite right by itself. The same is true for the title that will function throughout this book: the *pastor*. The title means "shepherd," of course, has New Testament precedent (Eph. 4:11), and seems at first glance to be innocent enough, perhaps even the best of the lot. Shepherds loyally care for the flock of sheep, feed the sheep, see them in and out of pasture. Only, what does this imply about the congregation that such a "shepherd" serves? In relation to the pastor are they only sheep, dumbly following, waiting to be fed? And are they gathered in order for the shepherd to fleece or slaughter them? Furthermore, the New Testament texts give a challenge to this title perhaps even more intense than that given to the other titles. In the Fourth Gospel, Jesus says things like, "All who came before me are thieves and bandits. . . . I am the good shepherd. The good shepherd lays down his life for the sheep. The hired hand, who is not the shepherd and does not own the sheep, sees the wolf coming and leaves the sheep and runs away" (John 10:8, 11-12). So, are pastors thieves, bandits, or hirelings? Of course, the image is dependent not just on the circumstances of ancient Near Eastern husbandry, but—more fundamentally—on the idea that ancient Near Eastern kings were commonly called "shepherds," and these shepherds did indeed often fleece and kill their "sheep" for their own benefit. But, the Christian tradition has asserted, Jesus Christ was a "king" who gave himself away for the well-being of the flock, laying down his own body as a door. For Christians, such self-giving is the nature of his "shepherding," the utter inversion of "kingship," and the breaking of the shepherd-symbol.

Pastors can indeed be thieves and robbers. They can be so not least if they take the title at face value, as if *they* were to direct the sheep, profit from the sheep, tell the otherwise ignorant sheep where to go, fence in the sheep so that only the pastor and the pastor's authority allow entry and exit. Still, if the title *pastor* is taken to stand for the work of a leader in the *Word-and-Sacrament assembly*, it can be astonishing. Such a leader is to set out the paradoxical word about a shepherd who dies like a lamb and then preside amidst the bath and the meal of this shepherd's serving, as if these were the very "pastures," "still waters," "table," "anointing," and "cup" of Psalm 23, capable of holding and comforting us all against evil and death. The faithful pastor "shepherds" only in a secondary sense, only by serving these things, only by carrying these things into situations of need, only by needing these things herself or himself. Trustworthy occupants of this office of leadership will seek to follow the model of the good shepherd's way, the way of serving and of the open gate, that the sheep may "come in and go out and find pasture" (John 10:9), that "they may have life, and have it abundantly" (10:10). But trustworthy pastors will always realize with both humility and relief that they are themselves not that shepherd, instead pointing beyond themselves to the One who lives at the heart of the assembly's symbols. Trustworthy pastors will be transparent to the one Shepherd. And trustworthy pastors will know that the Spirit of God raises up many people in the assembly with the gift of leading others to pasture and to freedom. Taking up the challenges and tasks of this paradoxical title, the inversions of this broken symbol, can rightly fill up a lifetime of good work.

So, quite aware of the title's dangers, this book will speak of the *pastor*. But, with ecumenical intent, the book will mean, at the same time, the presbyter, the priest, the preacher, the minister. And, in another sense, it will mean none of them, unless the titles are turned to new meaning in the assembly.

There remains yet one other title not uncommonly used for ordained leaders in current Christian communities, especially in North America: the pastor's own first name. "Pastor Sue," "Father Jim," "Reverend Mike," or even just "Sue" or "Jim" or "Mike"—these are standard uses in some communities. Such titles may be used by people who think that they are thereby avoiding the use of any symbols at all. Probably, however, the symbol resides in the very familiarity of the names. This symbolic use points toward a longing for intimacy. While the pastoral vocation of the one so addressed may be partly obscured, it is not at all forgotten. It is the *pastor*—the sign of wider connection, of God—who is spoken to as if to an intimate friend or family member. The *pastor* is made a pointer toward and a means of participating in intimacy as itself a holy thing; the pastor is thereby made into a symbol of one of current North American culture's most sacred matters. But such use also urgently needs breaking. Congregations and pastors themselves should recall Dietrich Bonhoeffer's warning (in *Life Together*) that Christian community is always mediated, never direct. The minister of communion and the communicant, for example, are indeed powerfully close to each other. But that encounter occurs as mediated through the bread or cup, indeed, faith says, through Jesus Christ in the power of the Spirit. That encounter always involves a wider community— "given and shed for you *all*," the old words mean. Neither the communicant nor the communion minister may further pursue intimacy, based on this important moment of mediated closeness, without danger of misunderstanding, betrayal, and abuse. Rather, the moment must be carried with great care, protected, allowed to be a symbol, received as a gift, and then let alone. The same may be said for other moments of ministry—hearing confessions and speaking absolution, preaching to a congregation you know, praying for someone in need, visiting a bedside, holding vigil beside the dying. The pastor is often admitted to a place of closeness; the pastor must know that this place is *symbolic, mediated*. Probably "Pastor Tim" should be avoided right now, much as "father" and "reverend," because of the difficulty in breaking the symbol in this time of erotic intensity and unrelieved literalism. In any case, any Pastor Tim needs to know that this title, too, is symbolic, full of longing for a thing that cannot be delivered by him alone, cannot be taken literally, that this title, too, is the wrong word and comes to its possible meanings only in the Word and Sacraments at the heart of the meeting.

But, in spite of all the difficulties with these terms, perhaps a particular pastor is a care-giving sort, a "pastoral" person. Perhaps that is why she or he found her- or himself drawn to this work at all. Or perhaps she or he is particularly intense or sincere or priestly or wise or approachable or friendly or serene or even dignified, seemingly worthy of reverence. Are these things wrong? Of course not. No more wrong than any of the titles we have been considering. Such personal traits may indeed be among the reasons that a person's social interactions helped to form the idea that she or he "would make a good pastor." Even more, such things may become part of the symbolic materials put into the mix of communal interactions, underlining the communal hope for wisdom or holiness or closeness. It is simply that they must not be over-emphasized. If "real" pastors are only those who are kind or pious or friendly or—you fill in the blank—then we are approaching the ancient heresy of Donatism: the idea that the validity of the sacraments is dependent upon the character of the minister. Rather, a responsible pastor will be learning how to value his own wisdom, while also knowing what a fool he is, how to value her own kindness, while also knowing that she cannot be the All-friend. A faithful pastor will be learning that she or he occupies a symbolic role that may be heightened by one or more of these traits, but that what the traits themselves point toward will finally be found not in the pastor but in the God to whom the meeting bears witness—and even then, often found only by faith, under a surprising form that is contrary to the thing expected. A competent pastor will be relearning the symbols. A competent pastor will be learning to live a way of paradox.

A Lifelong Catechumenate, Also for Pastors

Christian spirituality, at its best, implies a way of paradox. Of course, the word *spirituality* often does not open toward such continual relearning the reversals and inversions of the community's symbols. Rather, the word *spirituality* can sometimes be taken to stand for a series of timeless and absolute values that are to be striven toward and followed by the "spiritual person." Or, in contemporary North America, it may connote a personal interior state, open to religious experience and quite distinguished from engagement with organized religion. This book does not use the word in these ways. Rowan Williams, the Archbishop of Canterbury, wisely points out (in his *Christian Spirituality*) that Christianity began in an experience of "contradictoriness." The encounter with Jesus, with his preaching and ministry, with his death and resurrection, with the old Scriptures re-understood through him, so upset and reoriented human religious expectations and language that the ongoing history of Christianity has then continually lived with these reorienting questions. Renewal movements in Christianity—not least, the Reformation—have frequently involved a rehearing of these questions, a restating of the religious contradictions of Christian faith. "Spirituality," for Williams, involves each believer, day after day, discovering the implications of the religious questioning that lives at the heart of Christian faith. Spirituality itself—the "spiritual" in human religious categories and language—is thereby reoriented. Christian spirituality may then be understood as the continual questioning and redirection of human lives that occurs in the encounter with central symbols of the faith, symbols that live primarily in the assembly life of the community.

Such questioning, for example, comes to expression in Martin Luther's famous summary of the paradox-embracing Christian life:

A Christian is a perfectly free lord of all, subject to none.
A Christian is a perfectly dutiful servant of all, subject to all.

Especially when one realizes that this pair of assertions roots in other Lutheran and Christian symbolic paradoxes—"in this bath I die each day in order to live," for example, and "this bread is the body of Christ," and, especially, the christological paradox, "apart from this crucified man, I have no God"—the lines can be taken as one expression of Luther's *spirituality*. Another might be found in the deathbed note left by this reformer, professor, and doctor of theology: "I say we are beggars. This is true."

In our time, for another example, Sydney Carter, the Christian songwriter famous for "The Lord of the Dance," has framed the classic paradoxes, the classic Christian questioning of expected categories, in striking terms. His less well-known song, "I Come Like a Beggar," has the crucified Jesus Christ speaking:

I come like a beggar with a gift in my hand.
I come like a prisoner to bring you a key.
By the hungry I will feed you,
By the poor I'll make you rich,
By the broken I will mend you.
Tell me, which one is which?

And he goes on:

> The need of another is the gift that I bring.

And, as one symbolic place where such a gift is received and such mending occurs:

> Take the wine that I bring you and the bread that I break.

The images in the song come, of course, from the liturgical practices of the Holy Communion, the collection for the poor, and the sending in mission. But they come also from the Bible: Jesus Christ as poor among the poor, making many rich (2 Cor. 8:1-9); the imprisoned Jesus Christ as the key of David, who opens and no one will shut (Rev. 3:7); and God encountered among the hungry, the wretched, and the sick (Matt. 25:31-46). These images can be read into our lives, changing the way we may see religion, our neighbor, and the world.

Such working with the reversals and paradoxes found in the earliest Christian faith and enacted in the local Christian assembly—such working not only with the mind and heart, but also with our lives—characterizes a *Christian spirituality of the questions*. Indeed, Christian spirituality involves the engagement with the Holy Spirit, the life-giving Spirit poured out from the death of Christ, the very Spirit that makes chaos and death to be places of life, the very Breath that brings the dry bones of the despairing to arise, the Spirit of God's own reversals.

The pastor lives with the reversals and paradoxes, the hopes and the inevitable failures, of the very titles of his or her office. But these are only the beginning, only one sample of the larger task. If the pastor works with symbols and often is perceived as a symbol, then the pastor is invited to a lifelong questioning and relearning of these very symbols, to a *pastoral spirituality*.

Continually relearning the symbols: of course, such an undertaking belongs to all Christians. Indeed, one way to summarize the symbolic inheritance of any Christian, received at baptism, is to talk about the symbols that make up the "catechism," symbols that then may be reappropriated throughout life. Baptism gives the Christian this catechism as a gift. Conversely, the catechism—mostly made up of texts that function in baptism and continue to be used in worship— can be seen to summarize and symbolically represent baptism. Classically, the catechism encompassed a set of texts that together stood for the process of baptism, the process of anyone's receiving the surprising gifts of God and becoming a Christian. The Ten Commandments can stand for the beginning of this process: for anyone's first encounter with the idea of an ordered life in the world, free from idolatry. The Creed can stand for the community's handing over to the new Christian the story and hope of the gospel. The Lord's Prayer can stand for the new Christian's beginning to learn to pray together with the community. Then, especially in that shape of the catechism as it was formed during the Reformation, the texts went on: biblical texts relating to Baptism, the Lord's Supper, the ongoing life of a Christian, and the forgiveness of sins can be seen to carry the trajectory of the new Christian forward to the bath and into the Christian life. Note: the *catechism,* by this understanding, is not a denominational book of the right answers to questions people may not even be asking. Rather, it is a set of symbolic, largely liturgical texts—the Commandments, the Creed, the Lord's Prayer, and a few biblical texts central to the sacraments—that can stand for larger moments of Christian faith and practice. One old idea of the Christian life, then, involved the proposal that all Christians might continually relearn these texts, continually receive again their gifts, surprises, and questions, and that this might happen especially in the midst of the actual circumstances of people in their vocations.

Their *vocations*: the word has come to mean simply *occupations* or even *jobs.* But resident in its Reformation-era use is the idea of "calling," the idea that everyone is called by God for good work in the world. For Christians, that calling is linked with the call of God to life in Christ, a call that the Spirit makes to resound through baptism. For Christians, the call to love our neighbor as we have been loved, to serve as we have been served, and to work that celebrates the goodness of the creation itself, is never a call to abandon the world. Rather, the baptized Christian is invited to live the Christian life within the very situations of life and labor, side by side with everybody else and all the other living species, amid the struggles and the gifts of all the world. Furthermore, for Christians, that calling of the Spirit of God, resounding as it does in baptism and issued to every Christian, always comes as an invitation to encounter and relearn the paradoxes. So Paul writes:

> Consider your own call, brothers and sisters: not many of you were wise
> by human standards, not many were powerful, not many were of noble
> birth. But God chose what is foolish in the world to shame the wise;

God chose what is weak in the world to shame the strong; God chose
what is low and despised in the world, things that are not, to reduce to
nothing things that are. (1 Cor. 1:26-28)

The basic baptismal paradoxes include these: here, in this bath, we are united with
the weak and foolish One who is God's very wisdom and strength; so, here we
are put to death in order to live; here we are identified with the death of Christ
in order to be raised with him; here our dry bones take on flesh and are made
to breathe with the Spirit; here we are washed in a purity bath that makes us
dirtier—that is, here we are joined to Christ who is joined with all the unclean
ones of the world. For Christians, life in vocation always involves immersion in
these paradoxes.

Pastors also are baptized. Whatever the social and psychological origins of
their turn toward this office, at last they come to see that this calling as a pastor
is what they are doing with their baptismal vocation. Their relearning of the
baptismal symbols, in the context of their work with the Christian assembly,
is their own participation in the catechism that belongs to all Christians. First
and last, pastors too are among the baptized. Then their baptismal vocation is
specifically and concretely extended with an ecclesial appointment, a *call* that
the church publicly extends, a letter of call or appointment that they consider.
Among the symbols that surround a pastor are the concrete symbols of election,
call, vocation to the pastoral office.

Martin Luther, in his own vocation as teacher and preacher, understood his
need to be a lifelong student of the catechism, to read and recite and ponder
the Lord's Prayer, the Creed, the Ten Commandments, and, above all, to know
that he was baptized. Even though he was a pastor and professor in the church,
Luther thought he had to be always beginning again, learning with the newest
newcomer, the youngest child, the surprises of God's grace. He recommended
this same study to everyone else, in whatever vocation. Not least of all, he recommended it to pastors and preachers. His words at his own death—"I say we are
all beggars"—thus had an echo in his life as a constant beginner.

We will try to follow Luther's recommendation here. In the chapters that follow, this book will consider the baptismal catechism as one source of a spirituality
for pastors. It will imagine that the symbols rehearsed there need to be learned by
heart, encountered in their surprises and paradoxes, and continually relearned. It
will suggest that this can happen in the midst of the actual circumstances of the

vocation of pastors. Those actual circumstances include Justin's simple list of the presider's three tasks: a biblical sermon, thanksgiving at table and at font, and a justly distributed collection for the poor—preaching, presiding in the sacraments, and *diakonia*.

So the book begins with considering these tasks, learning them by heart like one learns the Lord's Prayer by heart (part 1). The pastor's vocation is found first of all there, among this short and simple list of the central things of the Christian meeting as they form the pastor's life. But then, the pastor too can find patterns from this common prayer of the assembly for the reorientation of his or her ordinary life as a believer, walking in the world (part 2). Let the summary of faith that is in the Creed, the summary of ethics in the Commandments, and the remembrance of the sacraments stand not only for the baptismal process, but let them stand for the content of Christian liturgy, of Word and Sacrament. Let them summarize the symbols that surround the pastor's life. While the reflections here will be necessarily briefer than the reflections on the central matters of the pastor's vocation, the book concludes with the ways these surprising symbols may affect the pastor in study and prayer, in daily living, and in dying.

The catechism—the ancient baptismal texts—and the short list of the pastor's tasks: these are one way to reconsider a spirituality for the pastor. In any case, whatever a spirituality for pastors may turn out to be, it will surely include the lifelong relearning of the symbols with which pastors deal and also, along with that relearning, the lifelong venture—and danger—of living as a symbol.

My wife and I read aloud to each other almost every evening. We have done so for years, rooting in a time when the children were at home with us. It is a practice that is very dear to me, giving us whole worlds where we have traveled, laughed, and wept together, while going no farther than our front room.

Right now we are reading Steinbeck's The Grapes of Wrath. Only a few pages into the book a preacher appears. Or, rather, a failed preacher. The Reverend Jim Casy had been a "Burning Busher" who used to preach and baptize, "used to howl out the name of Jesus to glory," and "used to get an irrigation ditch so squirmin' full of repented sinners half of 'em like to drowned." He does so no longer. He refuses to do so. But although he wants to stop, all around him is a community that still turns to him, asking him to pray, to have the right words, to bury the dead, to stand by the sick, even to hold something like a Christian meeting. In the end, out of his own wordlessness, even against his own expectations of himself, he oddly fills the symbolic role, first in standing beside the dying and the dead, then—by an act of ambiguous generosity—allowing himself to be arrested for somebody else. He refuses to be a shaman. He begins to be a man. Whether or not he begins to be a pastor remains doubtful, unclear, suspended.

Steinbeck knew, I think to myself. It is amazing how often one finds in fine literature that the failed pastor comes close to the task while the successful pastor betrays all trust. Casy is a not-so-insignificant sign for me of the struggle with the preacher's role, of the need to avoid lying and trickery, of the aching hope for integrity, and of the relearning of symbols. He is always thinking, figuring, until, in his silence and inability, he acts. I am drawn to him. I recognize the question.

Casy himself has ideas that he thinks have no place in any Christian meeting:

> *"I figgered, 'Why do we got to hang it on God or Jesus? Maybe,' I figgered, 'maybe it's all men an' all women we love; maybe that's the Holy Sperit— the human sperit—the whole she-bang. Maybe all men got one big soul ever'body's a part of.'"*

"You can't hold no church with idears like that," says Tom Joad, Casy's new friend and the protagonist of the story.

Tom is right. The Christian meeting does not just gather around general moral ideas about the whole she-bang or the universal soul. Besides the very baptizing and preaching and even shouting and singing from which Casy is turning aside, the meeting does, in a certain sense, "hang it" on God and Jesus and the Holy Spirit. But with what ideas does one hold a Christian meeting, then? And how can the very specific Christian ideas and the symbols that carry them include all men and all women, connect with real love, and avoid an immature refusal of responsibility, calling that "religion"?

In Steinbeck's novel—as, I must say, in my life—what a preacher is and what the meeting is for are linked questions.

I used to think that, in a certain sense, I could indeed be a shaman. I know that people often wanted me to make such connections for them. "He is so sincere," I might hear it said of me. Or, "he has such intense eyes." I knew that I wanted to give people more than sincerity or intense eyes, but I thought I could deliver that deeper thing for which I thought these expressions were reaching. I was wrong. Even real shamans have better tricks than this. And I am a Christian, for whom the only reliable connection is the one made by Jesus Christ, made in places where we all first think that God cannot be. I am a Christian, and that involves the trust that the connections that matter are made in community, not by me alone. So, let my eyes or my supposed sincerity be what they are. Let them add to the symbols in the room, perhaps like the color of the paraments or the presence of linens. Or let them not do so for those who do not like my eyes or me. In any case, they are not, cannot be the central matters of the meeting.

As I discovered more and more how wrong I was about the possibility of being a shaman, I found myself much warned by a saying attributed to Chrysostom: "The road to hell is paved with priest's skulls." And I found myself much comforted by a saying attributed to Augustine: "Insofar as I am a bishop [read, presider] I am in danger; insofar as I am a believer [read, member of the assembly; baptized Christian] I am safe." So then, beg God, let me know that when I rise to take on the presider's task, I do it from my place in the assembly. And when I am done, no longer at this moment called to the table or the pulpit or the font, let me gladly take my place in holy safety. That is, of course, not all there is to say about assembly leadership. But, for a pastor, it is an important beginning.

In his book, The Main Stalk: A Synthesis of Navajo Philosophy, *John Farella reports of several of his most important Navajo teachers, all of them former "singers" who could work the most important healing rituals, that they*

> *had been ritual practitioners prior to my knowing them, but they ceased to practice as they grew older . . . in approaching old age they confined themselves more and more to the "minor" everyday ritual acts that are primarily celebrations of existence—the use of corn pollen, the spreading of corn meal in the morning and in the evenings, and the smoking of mountain tobacco.*

I am taken by these old men, these nonpracticing shamans. "Insofar as I am a bishop, I am in danger," they might say.

In the Christian community, however, the ritual is made up almost entirely of "corn pollen," the seasons of day and year, the materials of existence. It is the story and the meal of Sunday, the prayers at the turning of the days, and the simple bath that makes us a part of this company. It is these ordinary things, broken into meaning by their juxtaposition to the surprising story of Jesus Christ.

I am a pastor. Let me care for these essential things among the assembly, like those old shamans using the pollen. God help me: the tricks and demonstrations of power I will let go.

PART ONE

Learning the Tasks by Heart

1

The Pastor in Preparing to Preside

The Lord's Prayer

Symbols and the symbolic acts surround and give shape to a pastor's ministry. Among those symbolic acts, one of the simplest and most straightforward is leadership in public prayer. Among those prayers, the Lord's Prayer takes a preeminent place. We can begin there.

"Gathered into one by the Holy Spirit, let us pray as Jesus taught us," calls out the pastor to the assembly. Or perhaps another introduction is used: "As our Savior Christ has taught us, we are bold to say," for example. Or perhaps the presider simply begins, enacting the confidence or the Spirit-gift called for by the various introductory texts. The assembly easily catches on that this is a communal act and joins in: "Our Father in heaven, hallowed be your name…"

Here is an archetypal act of the pastor in a local church: as the presider in liturgy, she or he begins an act of prayer and draws the entire assembly into its practice. The pastor helps the assembly to pray the Lord's Prayer. Can that simple act lead us into deeper understanding of the pastor's vocation and the pastor's spirituality?

The Lord's Prayer has been so central to Christian practice that it may be taken as a symbol to stand for all of the assembly's liturgy. It is one of the summary gifts of *Baptism*, a central pillar of the catechism handed over to us as we come to join the Christian assembly or as we rehearse, lifelong, the meaning of our participation. It recurs in every *Eucharist*, as the table prayer of the community, as the final text of the thanksgiving at table. It is as if we come

23

to the end of a presider's best effort—"praying and giving thanks as well as she or he can," as Justin would say—and we stutter out again "Lord, teach us to pray," using that beginner's prayer as the best conclusion we can give to our common thanksgiving at this holy meal. Furthermore, the Lord's Prayer summarizes our *prayers, morning and evening*, whether at the conclusion of a formal sung office or in simple family or personal devotions, reminding us in those places, again and again, of Baptism and of Eucharist.

We might take the *invitation* into this prayer as a symbol for the entire task of presiding, a symbol indeed that is an actual and significant instance of the thing symbolized. Pastors are ordained in order to preside in the midst of baptism and at the table. Their presiding can be seen to come to one important expression as they invite others to join in this prayer. Indeed, the invitation into this prayer might even be seen as a symbol for all leadership in the Christian assembly. The rehearsed voices of the congregation—the cantor and the choir—also enable the whole assembly to enter into central and known-by-heart texts and actions. The leaders of intercessions give voice to the communal cry for the coming of that reign of God which is the central concern of the Lord's Prayer, the coming of that time when justice is done and all tears begin to be wiped away. And the ministers of communion are actually passing out our daily bread. So, in a metaphorical sense, are the lectors and, hopefully, the preacher: we eat these words and live. The invitation for the assembly to pray the Lord's Prayer could stand for leadership in the assembly generally. Besides exercising that leadership herself or himself, the pastor may also be inviting the other leaders to learn the spirituality of the Lord's Prayer.

Could we learn something about what it is to be a pastor by considering what it is to prepare to lead the Lord's Prayer? *Prepare to lead the Lord's Prayer?* Really? Do not pastors know the prayer by heart? What help is there in that? But that is just the point. There is indeed help in considering how and why a pastor comes to know certain central matters by heart and how he or she then brings these matters into the assembly. Say it this way: the pastor knows the prayer and knows its place in the communal ritual in order to bring the prayer into the assembly. That is already preparation, and in such preparation lies a spirituality. Then, the pastor may think about the meaning of the prayer and imagine how that meaning holds the meaning of the assembly. That also is preparation and spiritual practice. And then, the pastor gives others access to the prayer, teaches it, passes it on, learns it again as in the lifelong catechumenate, uses the tensions and juxtapositions of the prayer precisely to enable such access. That, too, is preparation and engagement with the paradoxes of Christian faith. These three things may help us to think about the spirituality of the pastor: the pastor learns the important tasks by heart—not only the Lord's Prayer, but all of the central tasks. Then the pastor imagines the meaning of the assembly, using all of the central things to do so. Then, at every turn, the pastor tries to give access to others.

LEARNING THE TASKS BY HEART

"Learning by heart"—that is a remarkable phrase, probably deeper, more resonant than simply "memorizing." If you are a pastor, then you may need to let the text, the task, and the shape of the liturgical event and your role in relationship to the others—all of this —be imprinted on your body. Let your knowledge of the Lord's Prayer be a symbol here. Presiders need to know by heart at least some of the texts for which they bear responsibility in the assembly: perhaps, in the Sunday assembly, the opening apostolic greeting, the preface dialogue and the preface, the *verba testamenti*, the Lord's Prayer itself, the benediction, and perhaps even more. Even the variable prayer of the day, the opening prayer of the presider, summing up our gathering rite and foreshadowing the readings, might sometimes be memorized before the liturgy begins. We are not used to such memorization these days, but we may well consider its recovery—one small, steady task to mark our weekly Saturday preparations and bring us to the central themes of the lectionary and the liturgy for Sunday. There is a remarkable freedom in such knowledge, a freedom to begin to see that liturgy is not in the book but in the present actions of the assembly, a freedom to begin to invest the text with the gift of oneself. Indeed, if you are a liturgical leader with such a practice, you have doubtless found that the texts have begun to hold and carry you.

But an even more important preparation is this: if you are a presider, you need to begin to know in your heart—imprinted in your flesh, in the very way you carry your body—the deep structures of the liturgy. For example, you may come to know the simple praise/beseeching structure of the brief prayers of the liturgy—the "collects"—and, with that, also the slightly more complex shape of the eucharistic prayer. Then you may come to know the placement of the prayer

who will come and those who will not, to savor and treasure the importance of assembly, to learn it by heart—this also is a spiritual practice.

"Learning by heart," however, ought not imply that no new words are ever used. On the contrary. The deepest knowledge by heart will be the knowledge of the shape and purpose of the Christian assembly action. Then continual and vital attention to the constant task of translating, in company with all the church, will be one important way that deep structure is brought to expression and not obscured. Liturgical translation attends not only to the literal meaning of the words it is translating but to their function within the flow of the community's liturgy. We constantly need new texts that arise from that knowledge. And a pastor who truly knows, in the bones, the deep structures of the assembly may at last be the person who can pray the great thanksgiving at table "freely" and still be speaking the church's biblical, contemporary, traditional language, though that is a challenge to take up with fear and trembling.

Indeed, the sermon itself—a primary example of fresh words brought into the assembly—needs to be "learned by heart," though, here, this does not mean "memorized." Rather, whether one uses notes or a manuscript, the place and function of the sermon needs to be learned by heart, imprinted on the body. Pastors must learn the sermon's deep structure and its ritual purpose, its openness to the assembly and its fidelity to the assembly's purpose, its care and love for each one who has gathered and its openness to those outside this circle, its honesty and its lack of idiosyncratic affectation, its reception of the readings and its leading to the intercessions and to the table, its articulation of the whole flow of the *ordo*, its use of law and gospel. Pastors need to learn by heart that this is an act of love, intended to enable its hearers to trust God again. The very idea that preaching is part of the liturgy, subject to its principles and purposes, may be a new proposal to many of us, but it is very important and could be the source of renewal and hope in the face of the current American confusion about what preaching *is for*.

Perhaps what is meant by "learning the task by heart" and the spirituality it implies, however, is best conveyed by several pithy quotations from two of the finest thinkers about the art of liturgical leadership. Aidan Kavanagh writes:

> Ministers must not pose or seem pompous; neither should they be careless
> or seem to be self-conscious, flippant or condescending. They must be
> and seem to be completely attuned to the nature of the event and the

assembly celebrating it. A sense of natural physical grace in deportment, a sense of simple dignity, a certain self-discipline with regard to personal idiosyncracies translate into a general impression by the assembly of its being respected and competently served by its liturgical ministers. The minister at the liturgy, like a Zen-master, should be as "uninteresting" as a glass of cold, clear, nourishing water. (*Elements of Rite*, 53)

And:

The common end for which the diverse liturgical ministries work is not a ceremony but a corporate life in faithful communion with all God's holy people and holy things.... The minister, especially the one who presides, should know both the assembly and its liturgy so well that his [or her] looks, words, and gestures have a confident and easy grace about them. [A presider] presides not over the assembly but within it,... does not lead it but serves it,... is the speaker of its house of worship. [The presider's] decisions must never be gratuitous. They may sometimes be wrong, but they must always be steeped in a sense of reverent pastoral responsibility that is completely infused with the assembly and its tradition of liturgical worship. The sort of ministerial discretion this requires is a high art more important than any rubric ever written. (*Elements of Rite*, 12–13)

And:

To be consumed with worry over making a liturgical mistake is the greatest mistake of all. Reverence is a virtue, not a neurosis, and God can take care of himself. (*Elements of Rite*, 31)

And Robert Hovda writes:

The presider has a function with regard to the other ministers as well as to the assembly as a whole. The presider facilitates, discreetly yields the focus to the one who is operating at a particular moment, guides, prompts when necessary, leads the congregation in attending to the action. This is not easy for clergy who are accustomed to doing everything. (*Strong, Loving and Wise*, 19)

And:

The presider must be keenly aware of and thoroughly familiar with both the structure and the individual parts of the celebration. This is not the kind of awareness and familiarity that is gained by five minutes in the sacristy...before the service starts. And even the best "master of ceremonies" is no substitute for the confidence and assurance of the one who presides. (*Strong, Loving and Wise*, 26–27)

So, knowing the assembly and its liturgy, not consumed with worry, marked by simple grace, the pastor helps us all pray with confidence, learning the task by heart.

IMAGINING THE MEANING OF THE ASSEMBLY

But then we should consider the actual meaning of the prayer into which the presider invites the assembly, the prayer known by heart. Of course, often pastors, as well as everybody else, do *not* think about the meaning of the words they pray, perhaps especially such well-known words. But, if we attend to it, the Lord's Prayer, besides giving a model of heart-learning, can also provide pastors with an important means to imagine the meaning of the liturgical assembly. Indeed, we can find a central and summary liturgical theology by considering the prayer. Here again, this prayer may be taken as a symbol. The possibility of imagining what the assembly is actually *for* may be the most important preparation of all for the assembly's leadership, and thus a key to the vocation of the pastor. All the central matters of the assembly are also central resources for this imagining.

So, as a beginning in that task, consider the meaning of the Lord's Prayer. The prayer breathes a sense of eschatology. It is filled with petitions for the coming of the Day of God, together with some fear for the terrors expected in the last times. "Make your name holy in all the world, we beg you, as people see what you do," we may paraphrase the prayer of the community. "Let your reign come; do your will on earth as you do it in the universe." It is *God* who is begged to act in these petitions. The prayer is beseeching to God, not subtle messages to us. And the community also prays, "Do not bring us to the test," for we fear we will fail; and in any case, we beg, "deliver us from evils and from the evil one." All of these pleadings are turned toward a still-coming, hoped-for, feared event—the biblical "day of the Lord," the day of judgment, wrath, and salvation. But in the midst of these urgent petitions, juxtaposed to their pleading, are also two strong indications that the expected, longed-for Day has already dawned in the life of the community itself. "Give us today the bread of the feast before your face," one petition might be translated, indicating the confident trust of the community that God is free to make its meal in Christ already to be a beginning of the life-giving feast promised for the end times. And, when we remember that "forgiveness" was primarily a thing to hope for from God at the end, the other petition is equally stunning, equally celebrative of the actual *presence now* of that end: "Forgive us now with your final forgiveness, just as we are turning to each other, ministering forgiveness to those who sin against us."

According to this prayer, the community of Christians is, in very basic ways, just like everyone else—longing for God, in need of mercy, justice, and life, hopeful, fearful, likely to fail. Yet in two characteristics of its real assemblies—in shared bread and in mutual forgiveness—it trusts that God is already making it the assembly of the end time, the assembly around God's promised life-giving feast for all the world.

Both the theological and the ecclesiological bases of a healthy practice of assembly can be clarified by the consideration of that classic and form-giving prayer. Pastors may learn there again to understand the character and importance of the assembly they lead. We have seen that as one of the gifts Christians have from their baptism, the Lord's Prayer is repeated Sunday after Sunday in the Eucharist and every day in the prayers of the church. But we must also see that our communal insertion into this prayer does not distinguish us from the rest of needy humanity. Rather, the prayer in our mouths causes us to articulate with honesty the human condition in which we share. To pray the prayer of Jesus is to identify, as he did, with human need, sorrow, sin, and death. Borrowing the terms of first-century Jewish eschatology, we cry out our need for the "reign of God," for the day to come when God's life-giving intention for all things is openly enacted, for justice and an end to weeping. Yet, fearfully, aware that such a "day" will be full of "trials" we do not think we can pass, thinking that any such goodness must also be attended by great pain, we also beg to be spared, delivered in the midst of the horrors. By such a prayer, Christians stand with all humanity, in its need and in its fear. In such a prayer, the church exercises its priesthood for the world, making the "our" and the "us" of the petitions as broad as it can imagine. This articulation of human need before God makes up a basic Christian practice.

Let the pastors of the assemblies know this priesthood of the assembly on behalf of the world. Let them know with sympathy and love how they are not distinguished here from the rest of humanity, but are rather a voice of need and prayer. Let them thus know where they actually are and what time it is in the world. Let them see that an insertion in the actual local situation of their communities, a knowledge of the news, the ability to weep and laugh with real people, attention to such literature and film and other arts as honestly evoke current estimations of the human condition, awareness of the state of the local land and wildlife—all these are preparations for the assembly and its leadership, all of these are spiritual practices for the pastor, all of these accord with the spirituality of the Lord's Prayer. Then, let the pastors also come to the assembly as beggars for the sake of themselves and the world. Let them not imagine their vestments or their ritual practice as anything else than an underlining of the significance of this prayer on behalf of all the world. A pastor prepares to lead Christian liturgy by imagining, understanding, interiorizing this purpose of the assembly to be a priesthood for the world.

At the same time, in the heart of the prayer, we ask God, with an astonishing confidence—there is that word again—to forgive us now and give us bread now. Again we borrow first-century Jewish apocalyptic language, but here we find that language transformed, reversed. These things are the presence now of expected end-time gifts. Only God forgives, and that at the end. Only God will spread the great, life-giving feast for the called ones: at the end. Here, in the assembly, in celebration of the actual presence of these things, Christians turn to each other in mutual forgiveness, which corresponds to and receives God's forgiveness now, and the community holds a meal that it believes to be already God's meal. Christians dare to do this, of course, because of the presence of Jesus Christ in the Spirit, the source of forgiveness and the grounds of the meal. More, the assembly is then sent into the world to forgive and the assembly shares food with the hungry. The daily meals and personal interactions of Christians are invited to echo and extend the assembly, to become focused signs of the presence of God's life-giving grace.

So then let pastors know and treasure that bread and forgiveness. Let their preparations focus on these things, their bearing and their gestures attend to them, their music enthrone them, their planning allow them to stand forth in simplicity as the heart of the meeting. In the Lord's Prayer itself, these are the central practices of the assembly. Preparation for leadership in the assembly will be preparation to keep bread and forgiveness central, strong, simple, unobscured, clear, accessible. In such preparation—in such learning by heart—the pastor finds a gracious way to live, a helpful way to walk.

All three of the presider's tasks narrated by Justin Martyr—preaching a biblical homily, giving thanks at table, and seeing to it that the collection is distributed to the poor—come down to bread and forgiveness: "bread" in the holy meal, in the read and preached and sung Word that leads to the holy meal, in the sending of signs of communion and of help to the absent and the wretched; "forgiveness" in the bath, in the absolution, in the sermon, in the peace, in communion, in the sending. The bearing and stance of pastors, their words and the quality of their attention must show that they understand—richly imagine—these to be the central gifts at the heart of the assembly. Their preparation to lead must accentuate these things. Indeed, even the preparation of a seminary education might be seen as organized toward Justin's three tasks and thus toward bread and forgiveness: biblical knowledge, theology, and oral skill for the preacher; the knowledge of symbols and sacraments, their ecclesial history, and their liturgical forms—"by heart"—for the presider; and accurate and critical skills in social analysis and community organization for the one who calls for and helps to distribute what we call "benevolence."

Bread and forgiveness, the matters alive at the center of the Lord's Prayer, are "practices." They involve us in enacting the things that we believe God is doing. That enacting is first of all ritual, communal, repetitive: in the prayer itself, but also in ritual acts of mutual forgiveness and in the ritual meal. But then our hearts and lives are invited to follow—in forgiving others, in exercising hospitality at all of our meals, in sending "portions ... to those for whom nothing is prepared," as Nehemiah 8:10 has it. Such practices are nondistancing, nondistinguishing. They still do not separate us from the rest of humanity, the condition of which the prayer so eloquently articulates. On the contrary. They connect us, in bread and forgiveness.

So the *theology* of the prayer is this: God is the one to whom we pray, before whom humanity is full of both longing and fear. More: God is the one who in Jesus Christ has come to be with humanity, in its longing, need, and death. Since the prayer is regarded as being taught to us by Jesus, as being therefore an extension of his presence, its articulation of that human need is a concrete sign of the incarnation, of God's coming all the way into our needy death. More: God is the one who—in the resurrection of Jesus poured out in the assembly through the presence of the Spirit—has begun to give here both forgiveness and bread as a first taste of the healing of all harms. That Spirit teaches us, forms us to pray.

The uniqueness of the prayer thus does not lie in its use of the word *Father*. With that word, the Christian community simply joins much of the rest of humanity—for example, the ancient Romans who invoked *Zeus Pater, Zeus-Father, Jupiter*—in calling out to the divine. The uniqueness of the prayer is found, rather, in our having the articulation of need from and together with Jesus, before God and in the presence of Spirit-enlivened bread and forgiveness, thus in the *trinitarian* heart of the prayer. For this God is not three gods, but one life-giving God. Such a trinitarian theology can be seen as manifested by the three reference points of the prayer, all enfolded in the divine unity: God who is addressed; Jesus who teaches us the prayer of need; and the presence by the Spirit in this assembly of the fulfillment of the prayer in bread and forgiveness, the risen body of Christ restored and given away.

Leaders need to know this trinitarian theology and embody it.

The *ecclesiology* of the prayer is this: the assembly is the community given this prayer, taught it in baptism, repeating it at Eucharist, invited to stand articulately with humanity—indeed, with all things—where Christ is amid the loss and fear. The assembly is made up of ordinary people, people themselves in need but also people willing to stand with the need of others. The assembly is also the community which, by the power of the Spirit and the presence of the Risen One, is given now, as an earnest-gift of all that God intends for the world, the bread and forgiveness that the world needs. The assembly is the community, therefore, that confesses the enfolding presence of the triune God and is called to practice the word of forgiveness and the meal of resurrection.

The life-practices of the Christian assembly are then all like those of the Lord's Prayer: praying the prayer, being consciously present to and part of human need, knowing our need of God, waiting for God, yet tasting the forgiveness and bread of God's presence, mutually forgiving each other, holding the meal, finding its echo in all of our meals, bearing witness to God. For our meetings to be transformed into witnesses to the day of God, we do need to do something. We do need to set out the word of forgiveness and the bread. Pastors help us do that.

Leaders need to know this ecclesiology and embody it.

Pastors with a clear conception of the assembly are needed in order to set out the center of the meeting in strength, attend to the open door, help all—weak and strong, fearful and courageous—to come in, and set the ecclesiology of the Lord's Prayer in critical dialogue with local congregational practices. Leaders are needed to teach the local Christians what the third-century *Didascalia* (in chapter 13) called upon the ancient bishop to teach the congregation:

> Do not consider your worldly affairs more important than the word of
> God; but on the Lord's day leave everything and dash eagerly to your
> church, for it is your glory.... what excuse before God have those who
> do not assemble on the Lord's day to hear the word of life and to be
> nourished with the divine food which abides forever?

Indeed, in a time when meeting together at all may be in some trouble, leaders are called upon to teach and teach the nature of the assembly, the *ekklesia*. Leaders are needed to help the local congregation gather around those things that are worth running toward: not just ourselves or our ideas or our membership procedures, but the word and food of life, *bread and forgiveness*.

The meaning of the Christian assembly can be imagined and articulated in other ways, although, if they are faithful, those ways will be in continuity with the theology and ecclesiology of the Lord's Prayer. But the principal point is this: pastors prepare for assembly leadership and orient their own lives by imagining again how important the local assembly actually is, how its bread and forgiveness can hold us into faith and hope and orient us in a needy, beloved world. Then pastors may come with new love and confidence to their assembly tasks, that imagination having been inscribed upon their bodies as they enter into the community.

GIVING ACCESS TO OTHERS

But there is one more thing to learn from the pastor's practice of inviting a community into praying the Lord's Prayer. Another text from the *Didascalia* (chapter 12) may help:

> If a poor man or woman should arrive [in the assembly], whether
> from your own congregation or from another—and especially if they
> are elderly—and there is no place for them, then you, the bishop, with
> all your heart provide a place for them, even if you have to sit on the
> ground.

Here is counsel for the prepared heart of every pastor. Not only are we to understand our identification with needy humanity; we are actively to open the door to the assembly. Indeed, to turn again to the Lord's Prayer, the Christian history of the use of the prayer is also a history of giving it away, teaching it to those who are coming into the assembly, giving access to it to others. The prayer does not only give us words for identification with all the world's needs. It also gives us an instrument that is to be handed on—"traditioned"—to those who are coming to the assembly, giving the very least of them equal dignity with us in the priestly ministry of the body of Christ. Preparation for assembly leadership will always also involve helping to give access to the texts and practices of the assembly to others.

Learning by heart and learning the meaning of assembly must not lead to a closed door, to an inside circle of the knowledgeable.

One classic name for the practice of so passing on the materials of the assembly is "the catechumenate." Again, one of the major texts of the "catechism," the summary texts of the catechumenate, is the Lord's Prayer. It is the symbol and summary of the community passing on to come-who-may the deep structure of the community's way of prayer. It may be argued that some kind of participation in "catechumenate" always belongs to the ongoing preparation of the leaders of the assembly. Making the door open is an assembly practice, watched over by the ministers of the assembly during the actual liturgy, like the *Didascalia*'s bishop. Giving access to that open door is also an ongoing practice of preparation for the assembly.

What does this mean? If you are a pastor in a congregation, it is to be hoped that you are also passing on its texts and practices, teaching its gifts. Again, the Lord's Prayer may be a symbol. It is especially important that you are helping your congregation to learn and use the ecumenical text of that prayer—the "new" text!—since the older English translation is so misleading. Indeed, the ecumenical text is now more than a quarter-century old and it is nearly a scandal that pastors have not taught it, have not given access to its much clearer and more accurate meanings. But then, more extensively, it is to be hoped that you are helping the congregation to learn all the texts and actions of the liturgy, to have a sense of the Christian meeting's meaning and flow, empowering its participants to be skilled in its tasks, inviting them to see its connections to ordinary life. Or perhaps you formally participate in the catechumenate that is being recovered by your congregation, both for adult baptismal candidates and for the families and sponsors of infants. But, apart from these leadership roles, perhaps you are also sometimes *not* leading and, rather, sitting beside someone in church, helping them know what is happening, making a book or a gesture accessible. Or perhaps you are simply teaching the Lord's Prayer and the other texts of the liturgy to your own children or grandchildren. Or perhaps you say to a stranger, "come and see," and then describe the assembly and its practice a little, promising to help further in the assembly itself and afterward. In any case, you too, as a pastor, need to be making the assembly's prayer accessible. In so doing you will, among other things, be learning again yourself, coming again as a little one and a beggar side by side with other beggars and little ones. You will thereby be profoundly preparing for the assembly.

A principal of such teaching—and therefore of your preparation for the assembly—will be knowledge of the juxtapositions with which the liturgy is filled: Word and Sacrament, law and gospel, texts and preaching, thanksgiving and eating and drinking, the week and Sunday, teaching and bathing, the year and the *pascha*. These pairs are staples, of course, structures by which the liturgy is learned and taught and led. But so are the conditions of their exercise: assembly and its leadership, reverence and welcome, hospitality and holy regard, strong center and open door.

Strong center and open door: that might be one way to say what the Lord's Prayer itself images. Open door to the reality of the condition of the world. Strong center in bread and forgiveness. Open door in the priestly identity of the assembly for the sake of the life of the world. Passing on the skills of the community involves helping people know themselves as marked by both these themes of the prayer. And passing on the skills of the community is one important way to prepare for assembly leadership and live the vocation of the pastor. So "let us pray with confidence," as the old invitation says, giving others access into the heart of the prayer, helping others be held by the prayer.

But what is this "confidence"—even "boldness" as some introductions have it—and how does it relate to the confidence of liturgical leaders? Insofar as it is the stance of the pastor as presider, it is not flippancy, not *self*-confidence, not ownership, not supremacy, not even lack of butterflies in the stomach. Rather, it is the upright, open stance of dignity and love that belongs to one who may speak and enact the truth, God's truth, about the world and the assembly, the truth of Jesus Christ, the truth of law and gospel. It will be strong leadership, but at the same time, like all religious and ritual power in Christian use, it ought to be strong leadership broken to the service of the gospel amid this people. *Confidence* is the New Testament gift of *parrhesia*: open and bold speech, eschatological free speech, which paradoxically is the very quality of the speech the Markan Jesus, for example, uses to announce his servanthood and his cross (Mark 8:32). *Confidence*, then, is the leader's dignified love of the assembly, which, in turn, enables the assembly itself to stand in dignity and confidence as the strong sign God's Spirit is making it. *Confidence* is the assembly itself calling the leader again to the free speech of the gospel. *Confidence* is the Risen One himself, existing here, as assembly. It is the assembly, by the power of the Spirit, standing in the crucified and risen Jesus Christ, before the face of God, for the sake of the life of the world.

The pastor's preparation to preside can be a source of the way the pastor walks in the world. At root, that preparation of spirit is quite simple, as simple as praying the Lord's Prayer with others: learning the task by heart, imagining again the purpose of the assembly that prays this prayer, and giving access to the prayer to others.

But even more profoundly: your preparation for the assembly is always about your reimmersion in God's grace. The central texts and tasks you learn by heart, if they are truly the central matters, are all gifts from God, gifts that finally hold *you*. Then for you to imagine the meaning of the assembly is for you to be invited again to prepare to stand amidst all the others, as a beggar with the beggars, hands out confidently for bread and forgiveness. And then you are invited to give access freely to those things that you have also freely received. The practices of preparation in spirit are practices of grace, not difficult demonstrations of your own mastery.

I have quoted Robert Hovda in this chapter. But let me say slightly more about this remarkable pastor and teacher who died in 1992. Anyone who encountered Bob Hovda might tell a slightly different story. For me, however, this "presbyter from the diocese of Fargo," as he would call himself, was at least these things: the finest presider and one of the finest preachers I have ever known; an extraordinary custodian of words, even though he almost always spoke with a constricted throat and a half-growl; a serious pacifist, a Catholic socialist, a partisan of the Catholic Worker movement, and a man utterly unafraid to be out of step with regnant social opinion; a gay man; the steward of an honest and robust sense of humor; a fierce lover of New York City; a shy and sometimes difficult man; a recovering alcoholic; a friend; and, more than he would recognize or have patience for, a mentor for this Lutheran pastor and teacher. I mourn and miss him still. And I give thanks for him, wanting to name him here as I think about being a pastor. Pastors are not always simple, uncomplicated people.

I remember Hovda's eucharistic presidency once for a small gathering at the edge of a conference on worship in New York City, sponsored by both Union Seminary and the Riverside Church. Approaching the altar at the outset, he bowed deeply, kissing the altar in the classic Roman gesture. But then he turned and bowed just as deeply, just as solemnly, to the gathered assembly. After the mass, a large number of the very ecumenically mixed participants in this event stood in front of the Roman Catholic chapel where it was held, reflecting on Bob's fierce preaching and on his gracious, grave, community-uniting bearing. "That was church. That was our church," we all said, finding already there the Christian unity and liturgical integrity for which we yet long. Partly, it was that bow.

Then, I remember his attendance at a Lutheran wedding, taking place after a long history that included pain and failure and then joy after sorrow, more than a little of which history he knew. On his way back from communion, he paused in front of the seated couple and bowed deeply, in the same bow with which he approached the altar as presider, the same bow with which he greeted and honored the assembly.

I have tried to learn that bow. By heart.

It has seemed to me that Hovda's bow gave flesh to the wisdom of his writing, profoundly symbolizing everything he knew about presiding and being a pastor. Indeed, the bow represented what he knew about God. And it has seemed to me that Hovda's bow palpably enacted his own vocation and dignity precisely by signaling his deep respect toward the other, toward the center of the meeting, and toward the richly important and richly imagined assembly.

I have wanted to bow like that, both in the liturgy and out. Of course, it is hard. Such oddly formal behavior does not quite fit in our society, except as a jest or an elaborate overstatement. For Asian and Asian American Christians, struggling with the remains of Confucian meaning, it may even seem to edge toward idolatry, enacting worship where worship ought not be. Even the pastors or choir members or acolytes in North America who want or feel they ought to make some such gesture before the assembly's altar or cross, do so furtively, embarrassedly, a little afraid, with a half-nod or slightly stiff movement of the upper body. Not Bob Hovda. His bow was deep, free, gracious, more flowing than his constricted words could ever be. He was not worried about what people thought of him. And in any case, when it was directed toward them, people understood it.

People do understand it. They understand that they are being honored and yet that they remain free. I think they begin to see that the person who so bows is able to do so also out of a remarkable dignity and freedom. In the context of the liturgy, that dignity and freedom is our vocation as a gift from God, the very grounds on which we stand, into which we invite the others. We have been served by God's mercy in Christ. We are free in turn to serve. The bow symbolizes such service, a gesture that says, "The Lord be with you," even without the words. The inscription of liturgical meaning on our bodies, the imagination of the importance of the assembly, even the act of giving access to others—all of these pastoral practices come to expression in the bow.

Still, I suppose that it cannot much be done. That anxiety or stiffness will continue for now. But I still want to learn the gesture by heart, bowing in my heart when I cannot with my body, and sometimes—when I know the recipients of the gesture will not be embarrassed and may even themselves respond—bowing also with my body. In any case, the bow may be a metaphor for learning by heart, for inscribing the liturgical task and the liturgical text in my life.

On the campus of the seminary where I have taught for twenty years, Jonathan, a guard who is more like a great father of the campus than like a security sergeant, sees me at a distance, walking on campus. First, he raises his arm to wave, sometimes also his voice to shout. Then, always, he bows deeply, his massive, strong body bent over in joyful greeting. I am glad to see him, glad to be again in this flock for which he so passionately and freely cares. I bow back, as fully as I can. I hope I can be a pastor like he is a guard.

The seminary students to whom I am teaching liturgy gather in a circle in the chapel to learn something of the bodily gestures of liturgical leadership—walking, sitting, greeting, praying with open hands, paying attention. At the end and at my proposal, we all bow deeply to each other. Some of the students have taken to calling it a "Lathropian bow," mostly behind my back, largely with a smile. They don't know that it comes from Bob Hovda and—now—also from Jonathan.

2

The Pastor in Preaching

Word

B
egin again with Scripture. This time, not the Lord's Prayer from the New Testament and from our liturgical practice, but two specific texts that provide us with model sermons. Preaching belongs to the vocation of the pastor, and to consider again what it may be—what it is for, how to prepare for it, and perhaps how to live toward it—can be to consider the spirituality of such a pastor.

THE CLASSIC SHAPE OF CHRISTIAN PREACHING

One of the archetypical sermons of primitive Christianity is imaged in the story of the preaching of Jesus in the synagogue of Nazareth (Luke 4:14-30). According to the story, Jesus comes to the assembly, rises to read, is given the scroll of Isaiah, reads, sits to preach, announces the presence of the liberation promised in the text, and sets two other texts—about Elijah and the hungry widow and Elisha and the leper Naaman, thus about two outsiders—side by side with Isaiah. In Luke's narrative there then follows an uproar, a foreshadowing of Jesus' execution. Note, however, that in this text, just as in Justin's report of the Christian Sunday meeting and in most of our experience, the sermon occurs within an assembly, a gathering for worship, and follows upon and interprets the reading of a given lectionary text.

Yngve Brilioth, in his old but still magisterial history of Christian preaching (*A Brief History of Preaching*), finds in this Lukan account the three basic motifs (*Grundmomenten*) of all Christian preaching. In fact, he uses his entire book to trace these motifs of the sermon in Luke 4, critically but irenically, in their balance, their imbalance, and their development, throughout all of church history. Brilioth—himself a scholar, but also a pastor and a preacher—calls these motifs the *liturgical*, the *exegetical*, and the *prophetic*. So, in the Lukan narrative, Jesus' sermon occurs *within worship* (it makes up part of the *liturgical* event), interprets the given passage of *Scripture* (doing the *exegetical* task and setting the text alongside several other passages as well), and *speaks into the present* with divine and revelatory authority (with *prophetic* voice): "Today this scripture has been fulfilled in your hearing" (Luke 4:21). Of course, in the Lukan account, what would ordinarily follow such a sermon in the synagogue is interrupted. The Sabbath *ordo* of synagogue worship is not completed because the revelatory character of the sermon becomes an occasion of active un-faith and rejection.

If we set beside this sermon in Nazareth the similarly Lukan account of the preaching of the risen Christ to the disciples on the way to Emmaus (Luke 24:13-35), we find the same motifs, now turned toward the hearing of faith. With the "sermon" on the way to Emmaus, the Lukan pattern of preaching can be seen as archetypical for the church. In this account, the event does not occur in the sacred space of an assembly hall, but on the road and in a house. But because the whole event takes place on Sunday in a small assembly and because it leads to the "breaking of bread," echoing the basic *ordo* of subsequent Christian Sunday assemblies and reflecting the conversion of houses to the purposes of that *ordo* (a conversion concurrent with Luke's writing), the *liturgical* motif can be recognized, in its uniquely Christian form: preaching is found especially on Sunday, in assembly, in the house churches, at Eucharist. Furthermore, the *exegetical* motif is present in force: "beginning with Moses and all the prophets, he interpreted to them the things about himself in all the scriptures" (24:27). And the sermon is strongly *prophetic*, revelatory into the present with divine authority: "Were not our hearts burning within us ... while he was opening the scriptures to us?" (24:32).

Indeed, the presence of the same prophetic preacher can be an occasion either for offense (4:28) or for the meal of faith (24:30-31). In the shape of preaching presented by these two passages of the third Gospel, the encounter with the crucified-risen Lord in the meal and the conscious awareness of that Lord's presence in the word, in the one account, takes the place of the rejection of all outsiders and the foreshadowing of the death of Jesus in the other. In Luke 4, because the community does not wish to be among the needy poor, sharing the famine and then also the relieving meal with the outsider widow of Zarephath, sharing the leprosy and then also the relieving bath with the foreigner Naaman, they drive Jesus out. Jesus was welcome as "one of ours"—"beautiful sermon, Jesus! Aren't our children great!"—but not as the breaker of the strong boundaries of the meeting. It is as if, had anyone listened to Jesus, they would have asked how they might follow the sermon by sharing in Zarephath's meal or Naaman's bath, thereby joining those outsiders whose only hope is in God. In Luke 24, precisely because the sermon opens hearts to faith, it also leads to hospitality for the odd stranger, to the shared celebration of the life-giving meal, and to the running back to the city of death to tell of a new vision of the world.

Of course, Luke's two narratives must not be turned to anti-Semitic purpose, as if the church gets it but the synagogue does not. Many churches, down through the ages, refuse to see themselves as one with the outsiders, as beggars with the beggars. At the end of his life, Martin Luther wrote that astonishing note found beside his bed, "I say we are all beggars; this is true." But neither he nor most Christians always live out of that root insight. Many churches refuse to have their strong boundaries transgressed, even by Jesus Christ. And, God knows, many faithful Jews—like Elijah and Elisha themselves—stand with the lepers and the widows.

Nonetheless, the sermon of Luke 24 becomes a prototype for faithful Christian preaching. The purpose of such preaching is to enable and create faith. That purpose cannot be achieved by way of self-congratulation in Christian circles. The aborted sermon of Luke 4, the refusal of the gospel out of a desire to not be in need of it, remains possible, also in the churches. But in Luke 24, the sadness and loss of the disciples—but also, for the readers, the remembered narrative of the rejection of outsiders and the foreshadowed death of Jesus—are transformed by the presence of the risen Lord in the interpreted word of the Scriptures, a presence recalled, confirmed, and supported through the Risen One's presence in the meal. Both the disciples and the readers profoundly need this presence. The sermon of Luke 24 can and must stand side by side with the life-giving meal and, by implication, with the life-giving bath and the openness to strangers.

This prototype should also be read against a background in the Hebrew Scriptures. The very *ordo* of Nazareth and, especially, of Emmaus is found also, for example, in that account of the "great synagogue" that can be found in Nehemiah 8. There the men and women who have returned from the exile are gathered in the open air as an assembly (8:2). There the Scripture, the "book of the law of Moses, which the LORD had given to Israel" (8:1), is read. God is worshiped as present in this reading (8:6), and Ezra and the Levites give the sense or meaning of the text, so that the people understand the reading (8:8). This reading and preaching also lead to faith—or at least to mourning and weeping and then to comfort and great rejoicing in the strength of the LORD (8:9-12)—and to a meal shared with the poor (8:10, 12). The place and function of preaching in the *ordo* of Nehemiah 8 are exactly the place and function found in Luke 24 and aborted in Luke 4. Only now, in Luke, the Crucified and Risen One has become the content of preaching, the presence of the "strength of the LORD," the grounds of the shared meal, the one associated with the strangers and outsiders, and the source of service and mission.

These texts can give biblical resonance and depth to a reading of the two major second-century accounts of preaching in the Christian assembly. In mid-second century, as we have seen, Justin wrote:

> And on the day named after the sun all, whether they live in the city or the countryside, are gathered together in unity. Then the records of the apostles or the writings of the prophets are read for as long as there is time. When the reader has concluded, the presider in a discourse admonishes and invites us into the pattern of these good things. Then we all stand together and offer prayer.…when we have concluded the prayer, bread is set out to eat, together with wine and water…

In the late second century, in a similar explanatory description of the practices of the Christian assembly, a description that begins with prayer, Scripture reading, and preaching, and also continues with an account of the communal meal and food for the poor, Tertullian wrote:

> We come together for the reading and discussing of the sacred writings, as any quality of the present time gives occasion for forewarning or for recollection. In any case, with the holy words we feed faith, we set up hope, we build trust, and furthermore we close our ranks by the inculcation of precepts. In the same place also are exhortations, punishments and divine censures.…Certain tested presbyters preside in this…(*Apology* 39:3-5)

Here, too, though we may legitimately question and criticize what this old rigorist meant by "close our ranks" and "punishments," it is still quite clear that Christian preaching is an assembly-based action, that it is always intended to unfold and open the Scriptures that were read, and that it is meant to "feed faith" in the "present time."

Even today, the place of preaching in the flow of Christian liturgy, especially the liturgy of Sunday, carries with it some of this old meaning. The location of the sermon is not simply arbitrary. An assembly gathers, reads the Scriptures, and then hears preaching. Following this sermon, the assembly prays in intercession for the needy others and for all the world and then proceeds with the celebration of the holy meal and the dismissal to mission in the world. Such a location of Christian preaching—rooted as it is in the preaching of the synagogue and of at least the Lukan communities, discoverable in the second-century Sunday report of Justin's *First Apology*, and developed in the early centuries of the church—carries within itself an implied set of characteristics of preaching. A sermon in such a position must interpret the *texts* read in *assembly* so that the community may come again to *faith*, a faith then exercised (and further fed) in prayer for the needy, in the simple thanksgiving supper and in mission.

In spite of these sources and descriptions, however, preaching is in trouble in North America today. Perhaps this trouble follows from our distrust of authority of any kind and, therefore, our distrust of any single speaker who rises "six feet above contradiction," as some people have said about preachers in the pulpit. Perhaps the trouble roots in our deep distrust of words, used in our culture so frequently to sell, to garner votes and, as if by a widespread mutual agreement, to deceive. *Rhetoric* and *preaching* are currently not positive words. Neither is the adjective *preachy*. But at least one possibility for our confusion about preaching may be our loss of the sense of its place in both *ordo* and *assembly*, our loss of the sense that preaching is to awaken *faith* amid the real circumstances of the needy world, and our consequent tendency to use preaching like the old Gnostic-discourse Gospels (like *Thomas*, for example): Self speaks to Self about the religious or therapeutic technique for the well-being of the Self; "let me tell you about myself, about my experience." The point of those Gospels, of course, was to help individual souls to escape out of the world. Technique was accentuated, not faith, unlike the canonical Gospels where the point is much more to invite a real community of people to trust the action of God in Christ within the world, for the sake of life (see John 20:31). Recovery of the meaning of the place of the sermon, after the Scripture is read, in an assembly, to lead us to prayer and table and mission, may also help us resist the common malformation of preaching.

Still, the longing for powerful, communally significant, authentic speech does persist in our cultures. The sermons and speeches of, for example, Martin Luther King Jr. occupy a place of honor in the American national memory. So do two key addresses of Abraham Lincoln. People do still long for political leaders who tell the truth with integrity. How can there be public speech that is reliable and true? How shall we preach at the present time? Shall we give up on preaching? And, if not, how might the call to faithful preaching contribute to the shape of the life of the preacher?

It is at least worth consideration for us to place preaching again within the context of the *ordo*, within the event of the assembly, to see if there is help for us there. It may be that a careful consideration of our preaching task in the light of the pattern of preaching we see in the Lukan work, for example, may enable us to ask how preaching may encounter the current cultural moment. So there follow here, first, a proposal about the purpose and materials of current preaching, and, second, a consideration of the life of the preacher at the present time. When the preacher understands the liturgical location of preaching and its life-giving content, she or he may again find an appropriate stance of authority—combined with an appropriate humility—amid communal support. The spirituality of preaching is thus a liturgical spirituality.

THE PURPOSE AND MATERIALS OF PREACHING

Building on the work of Brilioth—on his liturgical, exegetical, and prophetic motifs—but considering the sermon of Luke 24 as well as that of Luke 4, we might suggest that Christian preaching should be an assembly-based event, a biblical event, and an eschatological event for the sake of faith. These characteristics flow from that *ordo* of Christian worship in which preaching participates and together they make up the purpose and character of preaching. The *ordo* thus gives preaching a role, a place, a defined and resonant task within the flow of the gospel-based events of the Christian meeting. The preacher who learns the *ordo* by heart will find resources there for understanding his or her preaching task.

First of all, preaching ought to be an assembly-based event. It is part of the liturgy, not something alien to it. It belongs to the flow of events, like the stranger talking to the Emmaus pilgrims and then going in to supper. It is an expression of the faith of the assembly, in communion with the faith of all the church, spoken for the purpose of grounding the community once again in that faith. While sometimes Christians have preached on the streets and in the marketplaces, away from the gathered assembly, they have usually done so going two by two, carrying along the communal presence of Christianity, and they have always done so with the invitation for the hearers to join the assembly: "Come and see!"

In the assembly, the preacher arises to bring to present articulation what it is the assembly is doing by gathering, reading Scripture, praying, and holding the meal on Sunday or on some other festival. Indeed, the juxtaposition of this sermon to the celebration of the Lord's Supper makes it most clear that this is a word that is to be eaten and drunk in faith, just as that is a meal that "preaches," that makes a proclamation into present need (1 Cor. 11:26). The sermon should say in words from the texts the same thing the bread and cup say in sign: "The body and blood of Christ, given and shed for you. Take. Eat. Drink. Believe. Live." More: the sermon should bring to expression what "church" is at all—an open assembly, with the word of forgiveness and the bread of Christ's presence at the center, available for the world, turned toward the outsiders and the poor.

Here is an exercise for preachers: Imagine that you have gathered with your entire family at the one-hundredth birthday of your great-grandmother. All the family, all the dozens of descendants of this woman—plus their significant others—are there. It is a great picnic, let us say, in a park. Then, because you are known as a good speaker, you are asked to say something to all that gathering in the park. Your task will be to bring the meaning of this event—something true about your great-grandmother, something true about the party, something true about the identity of the family in the world—to expression in words. The celebration will be marred by phoniness or lying or by talk only about yourself or your experiences. Preaching is like that. Only, in the assembly, it is the church's identity in the merciful Spirit of God and the church's open boundaries in the midst of the world that are being brought to expression.

Most usually, the presider in this assembly is the preacher, thereby facilitating the responsibility of bringing to articulation all the rest of the events in the midst of which she or he presides. In any case, the presider supervises the preaching that takes place here. That presider—and most usually that preacher—is a person who is in communion with the rest of the church, called and appointed for this communal, ecclesial task. And most usually that preacher is the local pastor, called here, engaged with this community, these people. Good preaching inevitably leads to situations of pastoral care, just as it also at least partly arises out of paying attention to the needs of life in this place. When the preacher is a traveler, a visitor, he or she takes the task, yielded with care and love by the local presider, as a concrete sign that this local assembly is in communion with other assemblies, including the ones from which the traveler comes.

The task of preaching thus ought not be seen as a lonely one. On the contrary, the preacher should understand herself or himself to be in a company of presbyters—perhaps the local ecumenical text study group, if nothing else!—speaking a communal voice, supported by the prayer and love of the church, articulating the "we" of needy humanity and the "we" of faith. The Levites, together, scattered throughout the assembly of Nehemiah 8, opened the meaning of the text and joined with Ezra in assuaging the mourning and weeping of the people. Tertullian said, "*we* feed faith," proposing the interpretive task as belonging to all the assembly, with a group of elders presiding. A bishop and a company of presbyters presided in many an ancient *ekklesia*. And yet, one person—or one person at a time—must arise and take authority to speak out of the Scriptures that the community has read, the church saying all the while: "And also with you! Amen. Amen." In this regard, all the churches can learn from the widespread African American Christian pattern of support and encouragement and participation with the lone voice of the preacher. That one person's voice must be honest. It may be fresh, surprising, personal even, not particularly cultic or pious, while yet never focusing on the self but on the Scriptures read in the assembly event.

For, in the second place, this sermon ought also be a biblical event. In the *ordo* of the liturgy—as also in Nehemiah 8, Luke 4, Luke 24, and the events described by Justin and Tertullian—preaching follows the communal reading of Scripture, most often in more than one text. Preaching arises following the reading of these texts of the assembly, bringing them to living voice, articulating their lively tensions as they are set next to each other, responsible to them as they are opened to speak of the Crucified and Risen One, of the Spirit poured out from him, and so of the presence and grace of the triune God. Preaching may take one of the texts as its primary source, but it will not forget all of the other texts that have been read, nor all of the witness of the Scriptures and all of the ways in which Isaiah next to the Elijah or Elisha cycle, Deuteronomy next to Job, Amos next to Leviticus, Paul next to James, the Gospels next to the Law, call for us to encounter the living God through the Scriptures, between the Scriptures.

The preacher ought never introduce a new text as "my text," as if the preaching event were something other than what the assembly is doing as a whole. Even Jesus was *handed* the scroll of Isaiah. In the Christian community, all the members of the assembly need to know the texts, own the texts, be able to prepare the texts.

Preaching is biblical. Augustine's great handbook for preachers (*On Christian Teaching*) proposed to teach them both the nature of biblical-symbolic speech and the use of rhetoric in expressing that speech. His intention was that preachers might be able to discover both what to preach and how to preach it. Authentic Christian hermeneutics, the search for the senses and meanings of the Scripture, the weighing of the biblical symbols, have continued to have a similar purpose: biblical symbolic intent in conjunction with assembly-based rhetoric. And yet, preachers need to be careful here: preaching is not commentary, not biblical lecture, not mere biblically influenced rhetoric. The purpose of the texts is not for the assembly to imagine how things might have been in other times, but to encounter the biblical God, the God who comes now to this time with all biblical judgment and promise. So Luther wrote (in *A Brief Instruction on What to Look For and Expect in the Gospels*):

> When you open the book containing the gospels and read or hear how Christ comes here or there, or how someone is brought to him, you should therein perceive the sermon or the gospel through which he is coming to you, or you are being brought to him. For the preaching of the gospel is nothing else than Christ coming to us, or we being brought to him.

Taught by the sermon of the Risen One in Luke 24, this intention of the Gospels becomes the pattern in which Christians read all of the Scriptures. God is present, addressing us, in these texts.

Thus, finally, this preaching ought to be an eschatological event, the presence of God to create faith. The classic Western liturgy has rightly surrounded the reading of Scripture with acclamations to the presence of God and with responses in the voice of the psalms. Preaching continues and heightens this intention of the

Scripture reading. Preaching brings this purpose of the meeting to direct verbal expression. These intentions point to the motif that Brilioth calls "prophetic," that is, preaching is to be the speaking of the living word of God into the present of the hearers. In the account of the sermon at Nazareth, the form of this "prophecy" was Jesus' startling "Today!" bringing to expression the nature of Christian eschatology, the presence now of the judgment of God and of astonishing help for the wretched. In Luke 24, the same "Today!" functions, now in the encounter with the presence of the Risen One in the very texts themselves, juxtaposed to the need of the sad and death-possessed disciples.

It may be that this prophetic task, this call to speak the very word of God, is the most difficult for current preachers to imagine in a democratic age. Preaching faithfully is indeed very hard. Easier, more culturally accessible options may seem to be available instead, tempting the preacher to turn aside to speak about his or her own story. Or the very idea of "divine authority" may carry a temptation for the preacher to articulate personal opinions as indisputable, even though a lot of pretense is needed to bring this off.

There is help in the model texts. In both Luke 4 and Luke 24, the form of the eschatological presence of God is in "law" and "gospel," in the articulation of local need and the proclamation of the presence of holy mercy, in telling the truth about death and life. A preacher does not need to pretend. What she or he must do is honestly speak of our common need and faithfully speak of the present mercy of the triune God. That is the word of God, to be spoken with authority, for the sake of faith. Then, astonishingly, taught by Paul and by the Fourth Gospel, Christians have come to say that the Spirit in the assembly enlivens the words we speak so that they bear witness to the crucified and risen Christ (1 Cor. 12:3; 2 Cor. 3:6; John 14:26), and that where that enlivened word dwells, the Father and the Son come to dwell (John 14:23).

Preaching is a trinitarian event: enlivened by the Spirit, the words of the preacher draw the hearer into the truth of our need, into the encounter with the Crucified-Risen One and so into faith and hope in God, into the communal life that flows from the presence of the life-giving Trinity. The preacher articulates, in the terms of the texts, what God has done and is doing in the cross and resurrection of Jesus, in Baptism and the Eucharist, and in the faith that these things sustains. Yet these things are not spoken as lectures on atonement or the sacraments or the Trinity, but as living words, participating in the realities of which they speak. Faith in the triune God, after all, is faith in God coming now, into the midst of our death, and making, *giving*, life.

Still, the rejection of the people in Nazareth is also always possible, the refusal of the surprising and merciful presence of God. The preacher needs to articulate the awful truth of human need, a need that many of the hearers may already know but for which they may have no words. The words of the sermon need to include the hearers together with all the outsiders and the sinners, using the terms of the texts as names for our sin and death and sorrow. There will be no insiders here; all of us need a word to say the truth about our common lot and all of us need a word in order to begin to believe again. Then the sermon will announce with strength and love the presence of the promise and grace of God, using the terms of the texts as names for the mercy of the Holy One. The words of the sermon will invite the hearers to come, to be carried, to be bathed, to be fed, to eat, to drink, to enter, to see, to trust, to be healed, to be raised, to follow—all of which are rich biblical metaphors for *faith*. Finally, this is what preaching is for: to show forth God and God's grace, in the terms of the materials of the gathering—the texts, the sacraments, the assembly itself—so that the assembly and each of its participants may come again to faith. The *ordo* of the liturgy will then move on to urgent prayer to God for all the needy world, to the actual meal of faith, and to the sending of food to the hungry and witness to the world.

THE PREACHER IN THIS CULTURAL MOMENT

So, faithful preaching ought to be an assembly event, a biblical event, and an eschatological event. Preachers can certainly fail in this vocation. But the biblical prototypes and the place of preaching in the liturgy will keep holding all three of these characteristics before anybody whose calling in the church includes rising in the assembly to speak.

The various cultures among which we live at the present moment, however, can indeed make such preaching a difficult task. It may be useful for the preacher to consider some of the current thought about the ways in which Christianity and culture relate and then take that thought to heart as providing insight both for his or her preaching and for her or his spiritual life. So, for example, the 1995 *Nairobi Statement*, published by the Lutheran World Federation, speaks of the relationship of worship and culture as marked by elements of the transcultural, the contextual, the countercultural, and the cross-cultural. As we inquire about the place of preaching in our own cultural moment, we may make use of this very fourfold schema.

Preaching will be transcultural, uniting us all across our cultural boundaries, exactly as it holds all three of the biblical preaching motifs together, in strength and in balance. Local enculturation of Christian liturgy—adaptation to a current cultural environment—cannot rightly decide to abandon any of these three motifs—say, to abandon preaching on biblical texts or to let the sermon bear no relationship to Baptism or Eucharist or assembly or to forget about the eschatological character of what Paul calls "preaching Christ and him crucified" as the "power and wisdom of God" (1 Cor. 1:23-24)—without also weakening or even abandoning the communion of the Christian churches. Brilioth's history gently traces ways in which preaching has sometimes lost this balance. American Protestant preaching of the early to mid-twentieth century, for example, can be seen to have sometimes lost its exegetical focus and even its liturgical setting, while having exalted, in compensation, the "prophetic" task. Much can be learned, even now, from the liberal Protestant address of the Word to the current social situation in the language of the time, but such "prophecy" could easily become vague, empty of biblical content, not "eschatological" in the sense we have been employing. In time, such preaching could come to have little left but a focus on "practical advice" or on the "self" of the "prophet." And, in fact, American Protestant preaching has been recently wandering, in search of a definition. But, then, so have we all. We need to have something like the gentle and catholic spirit of Brilioth to call each other, in all of our churches, back to balance, back to the transcultural elements of our communion. We will find help in this regard as we recover lectionary preaching and communal study and discussion of the lectionary—in the local congregation, but also in ecumenical study groups of preachers. And we will be assisted as we let our preaching always refer to God's action in Baptism and in the Supper, even if we have not yet recovered the weekly Eucharist.

So the preacher may know herself or himself as called to a transcultural task, astonishingly provided with gifts of mercy for people of every culture. The authority of the preacher arises from those gifts. The spirituality of the preacher centers in them.

But Christian preaching also is called to be richly contextual. The tools of this contextualization, again, will be the very motifs of preaching we have been exploring. A sermon will need to reflect and articulate an *assembly* in *this* place, with its transcultural Word and Sacraments, but also with its local forms of participation, its local symbols and language, its local art and architecture. A sermon will need to be *biblical* as it uses the best local translation of the Scripture but also as it continues the translation work, seeking for local images that carry the biblical meaning and function like the biblical images, articulating human need and God's grace in Christ through accessible local ways. And the sermon will need to be *eschatological* precisely as a speaking of God's living Word to these hearers, in this place. It will need to use patterns of culturally recognizable powerful speech to bring together the hearts of the hearers and the word of the gospel with clarity, dignity, and joy.

Note that the shape of preaching we have been discussing remains remarkably free. No strict interior design is given by this shape. Rather, the motifs of preaching that come from its place in the liturgy all call for localization. The communal participation in preaching may be quite vocal—with the sermon being orally encouraged by the hearers or interwoven with communal song—or relatively quiet. A local church might try multiple preachers or preaching as a dialogue. The place and posture of the preacher or preachers in the assembly needs to accord with a local sense of space used in the service of Word and Sacrament and with the importance, dignity, and communal responsibility of preaching. For example, the current tendency for some preachers in North America to walk around as they preach probably corresponds more to the democratic and chatty modes of television talk shows than to the communal centrality and dignity of preaching—while, at the same time, such a practice over-accentuates the person of the preacher. But the question is then alive: how shall a place of the Word be constructed in our communities now so as to be clearly perceived here, in our time, as central, spiritually important, open, communal? Furthermore, contextualization implies that the juxtaposition of human need to God's merciful presence, the basic juxtaposition of the liturgy, will need to come to expression in the sermon in ways that accord with local rhetoric.

So the preacher lives here, in this moment, at this place, among these people, all beloved by God. Such is the spirituality of a preacher.

But the sermon will also be countercultural. Indeed, since preaching articulates human sin and sorrow, death and need, in the terms of the texts, and yet finds those very terms converted into words for grace and the presence of the life-giving

God—since our death and failure is the very place where God in Christ through the power of the Spirit has begun to set out the life-giving fountain—there is a certain contrary character to all faithful preaching. The interior contradictions of preaching yield a form marked by antithesis: preaching is a "speech," yet it is also a communal event; an individual oration, yet responsible to and judged by a text and texts; a human voice, yet the living voice of God. Healthy Christian preaching cannot finally be culturally self-congratulatory, ethnically narrow, nationalistic, or jingoistic, if it regularly speaks of human social and individual sin and if it regularly announces God's eschatological, boundary-breaking mercy to Zarephath and to Naaman. The very words of preaching itself, the words of the Scripture continued and translated into the terminology of the local culture, will be "broken" and converted, bringing our hearts and our cultures along, as these words are used to confess our need and proclaim God's grace. The words of the sermon will be expressing our culture in need—beloved by God, but not itself God.

So the preacher's life, as well, will have certain countercultural strains to it. Perhaps simply being willing to become a preacher was already a beginning. In any case, the spirituality of the preacher involves continually inhabiting the questions, reversals, and paradoxes of the Christian life, probing the countercultural meanings of the basic Christian symbols.

Finally, such a countercultural stance may be assisted by preaching being also cross-cultural. If images and rhetoric belonging to other localities are sometimes carefully borrowed to speak of the grace of God here, preaching will also have a certain distance from "here," will bring to expression in the local community the wider, catholic communion between the churches. Indeed, the very use of biblical texts, from other times and places, and the insertion of those texts within the ancient *ordo* of the church—an *ordo* also arisen and elaborated in other times and places—can form the basic model for the cross-cultural work of the preacher. A North American preacher may be able to express more profoundly what the Scripture actually means in North America if she or he also knows something of what has happened when texts have been translated into languages expressing the Asian or African sense of the ancestors, the Aboriginal Australian or Native American sense of the land, the European sense of society.

So, to the extent possible, a preacher will also live as a citizen of the world, treasuring gifts from other places. The spirituality of a preacher has a cosmopolitan character.

Thus, the shape of preaching and its place in Christian liturgy can give to the preacher both a renewed and quiet confidence in the task and themes for his or her own life.

Once I was asked how I prepare to preach.

After thinking for a long time, I answered that I try to pay attention. That is, I said, if I am to be the preacher of the day, I attend to the texts that are going to be read, to the people who are going to gather and to the purpose of their gathering, and to the world in which they gather. I will be responsible, once again, to say what these texts might mean, who the people are, what the significance of their gathering is, and how we might see the world. I will be responsible to say these things together, believing that—in the mercy and presence of God—they belong together.

It sounds simple. It is not. Paying attention is not easy. I have found that years of familiarity or common presuppositions may have left me with a prematurely narrowed sense of what this Scripture passage may mean or who these people are. Attention requires me to see again the strangeness of the texts and the mystery of each person. Attention calls me away from a preoccupation with myself. Attention involves the difficult task of self-bracketing, even a way of self-abnegation. And once such strangeness and mystery are established, it is not immediately apparent how they fit together. How does an odd, ancient, Near Eastern text address these people, let alone the meaning of this meeting or of the world itself? Attention requires holding oneself in this difficulty for a while.

Because these texts are to be read at the Eucharist and because these people are constituted as church as they gather to do the Eucharist, the task of preparing to preach is deeper still. I am not going to give a public lecture on the possible significances of ancient texts for modern people. I am not going to expound my own interpretation of current events. I am to arise in the assembly to articulate the meaning of the meeting as an encounter with one another in God's present grace, believing that this assembly casts a searing, gracious light on all the world. If I am to be the preacher of the day, it is the faith of the church that is to be brought to expression in my speech. So I must attend to the mystery of Christ in the texts, to the mystery of the Spirit constituting this people as church, and to the mystery of the world as it is held in the endless mercy of the triune God. The task of preaching is, in fact, immense and ought not be farmed out easily to folks who just want to say something, without attending to that immensity. But, my God, because of the communal call to which I have said yes, it has been farmed out to me.

Imagination helps me to begin the task. Imagination can consider the strangeness of the texts, the otherness and surprise of the lives of the people who will assemble, the manifold variety of both the wretchedness and the blessedness of the world, and the resonances of meaning that will occur as Word and Sacrament are set side by side in this present world. Indeed, I need imagination and attention to reflect on how, by the power of the Spirit, the cross and resurrection of Jesus Christ gather all these things into the mercy of God, proposing justice and love.

For me, then, because I am a preacher of the church, continual practice in attention and imagination must be a part of my daily round. I read novels and go to a few films, chosen with critical discretion, so that I might imagine the situation of other people and pay attention to the ways fine artists envision the world. I read a little history and some ethnography, and I try to listen carefully to the personal stories that are told to me, not immediately imposing my meaning on them. I listen to the Scripture as we read it at our dinner table and to the great stories we read aloud before we go to bed. I watch the trees and birds outside my window. I walk on the streets of my city, watching faces, and I walk in the nearby woods, attending to the actual place on the earth where I live. In both places—streets and woods—I try to see what is happening. I pursue interests in other cultures than here, other places away from here. I go to museums and to art shows. I try to keep learning languages other than those I already know. I try to see if I can observe in what ways women and men, young people and older people, gay people and straight people may or may not differ in their experience of the world. I read a good newspaper, carefully and critically, though I do not watch much television, my feeling being that there is usually very little there that will surprise me. I read the Scripture alone, seeking to hold myself before Christ in the text, continually surprised by Christ in the text, eating and drinking the body and blood of Christ in the text. For me this lectio divina, *the "news," pastoral care, walking, personal reading, family life, and my personal encounters with other cultures and other languages all make up part of the preparation for preaching. Seldom do such exercises yield an "illustration" for a sermon. Rather, they function to train my attention and imagination. It is attention and imagination I must bring to the preparation for preaching.*

"But," my interlocutor asked, "what do you actually do to prepare a concrete sermon?"

I can answer that, though I do not know if it will be helpful for you. Say it like this: If I am to preach on Sunday, I read the texts on the preceding Monday. I get them in my mind. I try to pay attention to what is strange, to some odd thing that will not resolve, some puzzle. I hold all three together, juggling them, imagining how one of them might direct a sermon in a certain way. I try to learn the shape of the texts again, by heart. My intention is for these texts to be present in me, unresolved, as I go through the week, paying attention to the things and people around me and to our world. Our congregation now holds a small midweek lectionary study, after evening prayer, and I newly rejoice in listening to a few other people begin to speak about what they hear in the texts. And I go through the week, trying to pay attention, imaginatively.

Then, the day before the Eucharist, I make sure I have a few hours to pay new attention to the task. I read the texts again. I read them in the original languages and perhaps in some other language, so that I must read them slowly, increasing the possibility of being freshly surprised. I consult lexicons, concordances, parallel passages, and a few commentaries. And then I make my own outlines of what is actually in the texts, of words they have for human sorrow and death and words for God's grace and for the resurrection. I try to think of the congregation. To the extent that I have paid attention throughout the week, these people will already have influenced the way I have read the texts. Pastoral conversations will have put questions to my reading and proposed situations of sorrow and joy in need of interpretive images. It is not that I ever explicitly refer to a pastoral conversation or a personal need in the sermon, but attention to those needs teaches me again something of the shape of the human condition, giving weight and accuracy to my textual reflections. Furthermore, attention to my community, to the news and to the arts, will have shaped again in me the current aching questions of justice and injustice, peace and war. The texts must be seen to speak of the promise of God amid those questions. But there is more. I begin to see ahead of time the faces I will see when I preach, beholding in my mind their need for truth and mercy and hearing their prayer for me. I begin to hear these texts read not by me but by the assembly's lectors. I hear the assembly's psalms and hymns. Indeed, I check what they will be, reading the hymn texts as a source for further thought or for a possible image in the sermon, reading and re-reading the psalm as a text that may help us receive and sing the meaning of all the readings, especially the first. And I read and begin to learn by heart the appointed prayer of the day, itself a prayer that opens toward the readings.

It is at this point that what happens has everything to do with paying attention to the meaning of the Eucharist itself. What I am looking for is not merely a powerful articulation of the world's need or the world's hope. I am not seeking words for a learned expression of exegesis. Rather, I am hoping to find an image, a turn, drawn from the texts and responsibly using them, but capable of bringing us, my hearers and myself, face to face with God's grace. I am hoping to find from the texts a way to say how the death of Jesus Christ really is, now, our life and the life of the world.

But in the quest for those words, I usually cannot immediately continue. There is simply no direct path from study to preaching. I pray some, but then I have to get up. I go for a walk. I read the paper. I lay out vestments for the following day, concretely evoking the whole role I will play within the assembly. I talk with my wife. I try to relax my mind. I look at the images in my study or interleaved in my study books. I take a shower. I may remember some book I read two years ago or a fragment of an old conversation.

And then, usually, it is there. I return to my desk and quickly write the outline of the sermon. I check the transitions, think through the outline again. And I try to ask myself critically this root question: Does my sermon indeed say what the eucharistic bread and cup will say—"In the power of the Spirit, here is the gift of Christ that you may live. You are free to this life with the wretched and the poor." Then, since I preach from notes and not a manuscript, I transfer these notes to a little card and place the card in my Bible at the Gospel of the day in order to take it to church. That is all.

But that may be of no help to you.

This will, however: attention and imagination.

The other day, my friend Gabe wrote to me a wonderful letter in which he quoted his son quoting William Blake to the effect that imagination destroys tyranny. Tyranny defines truth literally, using that definition to hoard and distribute power. Imagination embraces the other, mystery, and the rich varieties of ambiguity. Imagination at least has the possibility of serving a community. Ah, dear preacher, here's to an increase of your quiet, lively attention and your rich imagination.

3

The Pastor in Table Serving

Sacraments

Christianity is not just an idea or a list of convictions. It is not primarily a religious inclination that an individual might have or a technique to equip an individual to engage with spiritual realities. It is certainly best understood not as a consumer good that an individual might or might not choose to buy in the marketplace of religious ideas. Pastors, thus, ought not be primarily purveyors of ideas or techniques to individuals. Rather, quite concretely, quite *physically*, Christianity is a *meeting*. Or, more exactly, the Christianity that is associated with the four Gospels is a specific kind of meeting: it is a *meal fellowship*. As such, this Christianity is an invitation for us together to see both God and the world anew from the perspective of that table, of that shared food. Pastors, then, serve the table.

CHRISTIANITY AT THE TABLE

Christianity came into existence at table. The earliest churches—that is, the earliest assemblies—seem to have continued the meal tradition of Jesus, the meal tradition with which the canonical Gospels are filled. "Look, a glutton and a drunkard, a friend of tax-collectors and sinners," went one old description of Jesus (Luke 7:34). Early Christian communities seem to have struggled to understand and to maintain Jesus' remarkable open commensality. The four Gospels written and read in these communities give central place to Jesus' astonishing, Godsignifying, religiously offensive, and politically dangerous eating and drinking with the *hoi polloi*. The Gospels grapple with his critique of the dining-room practice of the closed circle and his reworking of meal meaning. Indeed, it was at table that those earliest assemblies seem to have come to understand and trust that the now crucified and dead Jesus was risen. To say the matter with biblical metaphors, they believed that he was now among them distributing the bread just as Joseph gave grain and forgiveness to his brothers, assuaging their thirst as if he himself were now the water-giving rock. It was with Jesus' death and his presence among them at table that they came to believe this word: "I am among you as one who serves" (Luke 22:27).

"Who is greater," they came to say that he had asked, "the one who reclines or the one who serves the food?" Surely you know, the question implies. You understand the power that is expressed at virtually all tables, understand the cultural form of that power as it was enacted at the time. The greatest is, of course, anyone among the elite who reclines, anyone who is served. Such a person is far greater than the slaves and the women, the children and the prostitutes, who come in and out on the fourth side of the *triclinium*, that ancient three-sided dining room, to put food on the tables of the reclining rich. Such a person is far greater than the low-class table servers, table entertainers, and forced table companions who would never recline at their own table. "But," the Crucified-Risen One now says, "I am among you as a *diakonos*, as one who serves the food at table. I am among you, reversing all values, like a master who has his slaves recline and girds himself to serve their table" (See Luke 12:37).

So great was this Christian critique of the dining room—like Paul's explicit critique in the first letter to the Corinthians (1 Corinthians 11)—that such closed-circle reclining slowly disappeared in the meetings of the Christian assembly. But *serving food* did not. Everyone in the growing assembly stood. The distinction between eaters and servers declined. But there were still table servers: they were now the very leaders of the assemblies. A small table was brought into the midst of an increasingly larger room. Food was set out. Thanksgiving was given. The shared loaf and the common cup that usually framed a festive meal were accentuated, so much so that all the other food could finally be given away as table service to the poor and hungry of the world, so much so that, when forced by persecution and state pressure, the community could move the bread and the cup and the collection for the poor to a morning meeting.

Christianity came into existence as a meal fellowship. Biblical images, some of them used in the early centuries of the faith, can help us understand the importance of this assertion. The food itself was now the very presence of Jesus, his encounterable body in our midst, his covenant-making blood on the lintels of our bodies. The meal was the taste of the feast on the mountain (Isaiah 25), the Spirit-given end of death itself, the gathering of all peoples to eat and drink, like Abraham and Sarah (Genesis 18), with the Holy Trinity. The gathering was now the *qahal*, the *ekklesia*, eating and drinking with God and sending portions to those for whom nothing was prepared, as in the account of Nehemiah (Nehemiah 8).

More: the bath that we call baptism functioned as a washing that joined people to this meal-company. Of course, it was a birth-through-water to a new reality, a passage to life by immersion in death, but it was that precisely by being a bathing-before-the-meal, a kind of ancient washing-up. Sunday came to be the communal meal-keeping day, the Lord's Day because it was the day of the Lord's Supper. Even the Scripture read in the assembly and the words of the preaching were a feast, words to eat, like a scroll covered with lamentation and mourning and woe—with the death of Christ and the truth of our need—and yet given to eat, sweet and life giving, the very feast of God (Ezek. 2:8—3:3) and food of the Spirit. Indeed, the words as well were to be *served* up, like food, like Bread of Life, by table servers of the Word, as the Twelve call themselves, according to Acts (6:4; cf. 1:17, 24), by table servers of the word of God's reconciliation with the world, as Paul calls himself in 2 Corinthians (5:18-19).

This table fellowship continued. It was because it was seen as a dangerous supper club that the Roman governor Pliny and the emperor Trajan tried to suppress Christianity in the early second century. It was as a host at table—and as one gifted for prayer at table, for table service—that old Bishop Polycarp came into view in the account of his martyrdom, also from the second century. In the same century, as we have seen, Justin concluded his defense of the faith with a hugely important meal account. Christians remind each other that they are baptized, he wrote to the emperor Antoninus Pius, by repeatedly meeting together, by giving thanks over what they eat, and by sharing that food with the hungry and the poor. The Sunday meeting for word and table, received from Jesus the crucified and celebrating both God's creation and Jesus' resurrection, was the preeminent example of such repeated meeting, such thanksgiving over food, such sending of food into the hungry streets and wretched prisons of Rome. Indeed, it is important to note that, for Justin as for many in the ancient church, baptism and the meal-meeting and the community's identity, its witness and its service all flow together. Numbering the sacraments, counting them as discrete phenomena can mislead us here. We may do better by considering a sacramental singleness: the bath leads to the meal; the meal and the sending to the poor recall the bath. Such, at least, was Justin's testimony to the emperor.

No wonder, then, that house churches were especially remodeled to make room for the communal feast and, sometimes, to make room for the bath before the feast. Then, when Christians came to use the great public buildings of the empire, called *basilicas*, those buildings were reoriented to godly purpose by placing a table in the midst, on the pavement, among the people. While the ancient bishops may have arrived in such a room with ceremony befitting imperial magistrates, ceremony borrowed from imperial court ritual—with attendants and incense, standards and torches—for centuries those same bishops then continued by doing what Christian leaders most characteristically do: serving food from the table. The bishops enacted domestic service, like table hosts, thereby utterly refocusing a new kind of imperial meaning around the meal of Christ given away to the whole assembly, around leaders who serve, and around significant relief for the poor. Bishops may have sometimes *looked* like magistrates, but they *served*. And they were especially assisted not by courtiers and bureaucrats and guards, but by people who came to be called *deacons*, people who brought to expression and assisted in the vocation of the bishop to serve at the table of the Word, the table of the Eucharist, and the table of the poor.

Here, then, is a useful thing for us to note, a fragment from the past that floats down to us now amid the flotsam of oddities in the various streams of time that make up history. Here is a gift that may surprise us into seeing anew an image we may actually use: Christianity came into existence as a meal fellowship.

When it is healthy, Christianity is a meal fellowship still.

If you have participated even slightly in the liturgical movement, then you have joined in the recovery of this meal: Eucharist every Sunday as the principal service of the congregation; the altar called a table and placed more and more clearly in our midst; the Word of God read and preached in juxtaposition to the gift of this table, from a reading desk set strongly amidst the community of this table; preaching interpreting the Word in the light of the table; indeed, the table of the Word itself set with richer fare, as the lectionary has drawn more extensively from the whole banquet of the Scriptures. These have been themes of that movement throughout the twentieth century. These themes are important not just as historical recoveries, but because the gospel itself is a life-giving Bread and a saving Drink. These table-renewal themes are important because the identity of Jesus Christ and the meaning of his death are given and known in his meal gift—"My body for you; my blood of the new covenant." Indeed, they are important because the Holy Trinity itself is like that expression of Catherine of Sienna—"our Table, our Food, and our Waiter"—or like that icon of Andrei Roublev: Abraham and Sarah's three guests around the cup, with room for us all at the table.

Such theological seriousness led to yet further table themes in the liturgical movement of the late twentieth century. At least there have been these: baptism as introduction into the community of the table and the table as the continual remembrance that we are baptized; candidates for baptism learning to join the community in feeding the poor; the whole baptized assembly—children and adults, rich and poor, firm and infirm, insiders and outsiders—as welcome to the table; the food of the table as genuinely shared food—a common loaf, a shared cup; this beautiful but simple food set out, held and consumed with great reverence; stronger and stronger thanksgivings at table, the presider truly giving thanks as well as she or he can, drawing all of us into the thanksgiving; the food of this thanksgiving table taken away in haste and love to those of the community who cannot be here because they are sick or in prison or engaged in communally important work; the Easter vigil recovered as a night annually accenting the central importance of the stories and the bath that lead us to the life-giving table; and the urgent, visible unity between Christians as unity at this table, as "full communion." These themes for renewal are not gone, nor are they fully achieved. But note: they are table themes, meal-keeping themes.

Now, in our twenty-first century, the liturgical movement has recovered yet further themes around the table, ancient and still crucial themes: the collection at the table becoming genuinely a collection for the hungry and the poor, as already Paul and Justin knew; the food of the table, the bread and cup, witnessing to the goodness of creation and to our inseparable engagement with the well-being of the earth, as already Irenaeus knew; the economy of the table, the economy of both abundance and of "just enough" for everybody who is there, the economy of sustainable consumption, as an economic proposal to the world, as already Ambrose and Chrysostom—and also Benedict—knew; and the very community of those who eat and drink at the table being now sent away as itself the Body of Christ, formed by the Spirit and given away to our neighbors in the world, as already Ignatius and Polycarp and Augustine—but also Luther—knew.

So we might try saying it this way: Christianity is a meal fellowship. The meal of the Word, the Word of the meal is itself a witness to the world of God's love for the world, is itself the very mission of God in the world.

PASTORS AS TABLE SERVERS

But if this is true, then a particular thing needs to be said about the form of leadership in Christian communities. There are lots of patterns for religious leadership in the world that are not appropriate for Christian purposes. Christian leaders are not to be judges or shamans, though we may have seen some interesting points of comparison between these functions and the work of Christian elders and priests. Christian leaders certainly are not to be monarchs or hierarchs, potentates or princes. Or, in a more modern version of such power, they are not to be licensed deliverers of unchallenged monologues on subjects of their own choosing. Nor are they to be talk-show hosts or celebrities or entertainers.

Rather, Christianity is a meal fellowship, and Christian leaders are table servers.

It is fascinating that the privileged New Testament words for "ministry," "minister," and "to minister" are *diakonía*, *diákonos*, and *diakonéo*: "table service," "table server," and "to serve food," in their basic meanings. Certainly, other words than this relatively rare—even *odd*—set were available for leadership and office in a religious or a secular community in the first century. But these are the words that were centrally used in much of Christianity, in the Gospels and in the Pauline epistles. While this complex of words comes to mean simply "service" or even "office of service," the concrete meaning of actually serving at table continues to echo in all their figurative, abstract, and metaphoric meanings. So, while we may translate Acts 6:4 to the effect that the Twelve want to devote themselves "to prayer and to serving the word," we may lose the sense—present in the Greek— that the Twelve want to serve the Word as food is served to a meal-community. At the center of the meaning of the *diakonía*-complex is always the setting out of food or, in a wider sense, the giving way of concrete relief, as food to the poor. That connotation hovers about in any use of these words.

"Minister," "ministry," "to minister"—this complex of English words, originating in Latin, certainly did once carry the same connotation. "To minister" was once, primarily, "to set our food." But such a sense has practically disappeared, the concrete meaning no longer echoing in its religious or political use. "Ministers" hardly are servers any more. They are, rather, high governmental officers or, as religious figures, they can be hierarchs, addressed with the title "Reverend" or "Most Reverend." Or, more recently, they are suspected figures who may have misused their power, sexually, religiously, or politically.

We would do well to recover the concrete meaning and the concrete connotations of "ministry." Let the ministers be *diákonoi*. Let the gospel be set out *as* food, *in* the food, and *in the relief* to the poor. Christianity is a meal fellowship and *diakonía* is its unique idea about leadership. The words for this recovery, of course, are words from the heart of the Gospel tradition: "Whoever wants to be first must be last of all and table server of all" (Mark 9:35) and "Whoever wishes to become great among you must be your table server, and whoever wishes to be first among you must be slave of all. For the Son of Man came not to be served at table but to serve the table, and to give his life a ransom for the many" (Mark 10:43-45). Finally, the great table service of Christ to the world is the cross. There, by holy mercy, he is the server and the food, the very fruit from the tree of life for faith to receive and eat and live and also the very famine relief of God served up to all the needy world.

But, formed by the Spirit poured out from his cross and resurrection, we too may serve this table. Our service may be like that of Peter's mother-in-law (Mark 1:29) or of the women who followed Jesus (Mark 15:40-41; Matt. 27:55; Luke 8:3) or of Martha who set that table in Bethany (John 12:2). In the Gospel books, it is only Jesus and the women—and the angels, in Mark and Matthew—who get it about service. It is as if the men have read Plato (*Gorgias* 491e): "How can a man be happy when he has to serve someone?" What belongs to a man is ruling, not serving. The Gospel tradition directly counters this proposal. So, going the way of Jesus and of the Gospel women, our service may be like Paul, who served up the word of reconciliation (2 Cor. 5:18-19) while he was also collecting the relief—the table service—to take to the poor of Jerusalem (2 Cor. 8:4; 9:1, 12-13; Rom. 15:25, 31). Or it may be like the seven, who according to Acts did serve food tables and distribute relief, as well as like the Twelve who served the table of the Word (Acts 6; cf. 1:17, 25). Or it may be like that of the angels themselves, who came to the fasting Christ in the wilderness and set out food to him there (Mark 1:13).

But "ministry" will be table service.

It then follows that the concern of ministry will be to serve not just any food, but to set out, in holy service to the gathered assembly, the *gospel* of Jesus Christ. The concern of ministry will be to set out that gospel in words that are like the bread and the cup of the Eucharist, in the bread and cup themselves, and in bread given to the hungry. As we have seen, these three tasks were the focused role of the presider in Justin's second-century assembly. These same tasks draw our attention now as we consider the pastor's role: to preach a sermon from the texts, serving the food of the Word we might say; to give thanks as well as possible, serving the table; and to see to it that the collection is distributed to the wretched and the hungry. All three are table service.

Thought of as *diakonia*, as table-serving ministry, these tasks of the assembly's presider ought still be held together. In the leadership of a particular Sunday meeting, they should be only rarely parsed out to different persons. The presider and preacher is usually one-in-the-same person, and that person also directs our attention to a hungry world. Then the preacher of law and gospel will also be the leader of thanksgiving and beseeching at the table, and also the presider in the midst of the amazing commerce that seeks to give away signs of hope and life to our neighbors in the world.

Sometime, dear pastor, when you are alone in the place where your assembly meets, here is an exercise for you. Stand at the ambo of your community for a moment. Then stand at the table of thanksgiving. Then stand at the door. And, as introduction to all three and as their constant ground, stand at the font. Consider your remarkable vocation, your important office of immense love. Again and again, learn the three tasks by heart.

Still, all of us are involved in each of the three tasks, the presider simply exercising serving leadership in our opening the Word, our giving thanks and helping each other to eat and drink, and our sending and being sent to those in need. Thought of as *diakonia*, as table-serving ministry, the authority of the preacher should be seen simply as the awesome authority of one beggar giving other beggars bread in a hungry world. If it is not really the bread of Christ that he or she is giving out, then it is no authority. The point of this preaching is that the assembly should eat and drink—both here in the words and in the Supper itself—and so come to trust God again as the giver of the Bread of Life exactly in those places where we have only known death. The preaching is to be famine relief. So is the Supper, the Eucharist, the Mass. At the table, in the unity of the Spirit, through and with Jesus Christ, the presider is to lead us in proclaiming with thanksgiving how God gives life where we find only death, and then she or he is to see to it that even the least one in the assembly is served with the food of this trinitarian thanksgiving. Preaching is to lead us to the Supper as to the visible Word and then invite us to turn in faith toward the famine in the rest of the world—begging for and signing God's great relief in the prayers of intercession, in the collection, and in the sending. The collection and sending of food and money are also famine relief, *diakonía*, and the presider is to see to their faithful distribution.

Ordained ministry is table service. That is why we ordain people. We train them. We invite them to come deeper into the life-giving meaning and the world-reversing discipline of the gospel table. We urge them to consider and interiorize the paradox that we seek to have strong leaders who are table servers. Then, at the invitation of a concrete assembly and in communion with as much of the church as possible, we pray for them to be used by the Spirit in the life-giving order of the table: gathering, word, meal, sending.

Of course, this table service of the gospel does not just belong to the ordained. There are rightly many ministries—many table services—in the assembly of God. Their diversity expresses the rich variety of the gifts of God and the rich diversity of the assembly itself. Their common work at the table expresses the assembly's unity. Presiding—focusing a participating meeting on the table of the Word, table of the Eucharist, table of the poor—is indeed one of the services deeply needed by the assembly. There are many others. Cantors and readers and intercessors and communion servers and doorkeepers and bread bakers and altar-guild members are also table servers. So are catechists and sponsors who lead catechumens through the bath to the table, as well as teachers who help us reflect on the meaning of the table and deacons who distribute the collection from the table and visitors who care for those separated from the table and social activists who, sent by the assembly's sending, fight for the justice of the table in the world. So are all of us together, sent as food to our neighbors.

Here, too, it is not just any food these many ministers are invited to set out. It is the gospel of Jesus Christ, set out like food on the table of the Word, the table of the Eucharist, the table of the poor. Take the example of the table service, the ministry, the *diakonía* of the cantor. Say it first negatively: Cantors, too, are not to be licensed deliverers of unchallenged musical monologues or choral numbers on themes of their own choosing. That would be to take the way of unbroken power. "It shall not be so among you." Rather, they are to help us sing around the table—around the gathering to the table that is the bath of baptism, around the table of the Word, around the table of the Eucharist, and around the sending to the table of the poor. They help us sing around the gospel in these places, help us sing the gospel of Jesus Christ to each other. That is their service. With their own bodies, with their own voices and hands, and together with the choir—the rehearsed voices of the assembly—they are to help us do the whole table-*ordo* together, in harmony, in dissonance and resolved dissonance, communally, beyond ourselves, praise-fully, woe-fully, *musically*. We sing at this table of Christ. And cantors help us. We could say something like the same thing about each of the various ministries.

A special concern might be expressed for that ministry actually named "diaconal ministry" or the "office of the deacon." In fact, there is something uniquely, surprisingly Christian about having an office called "deacon" or "table server." There is also something confusing about it, since "ministry," *diakonía*, "table service," belongs to each of the various leaders of the assembly. There is also a ministry, a *diakonía* of the whole people of God. Still, insofar as deacons or diaconal ministers bring the vocation of a bishop or of the whole church to focused expression, proclaiming the gospel at the table of the Word, serving the cup at the table of the Eucharist, and distributing at least some of the collection of the church at the table of the poor, their office can be a refreshing and remarkable gift. They can remind us of the table vocation of us all, the table character of the whole Christian movement. But, if the office of deacon supplants other legitimate ministries, always setting aside lay assisting ministers in the liturgy, for example, or if deacons become the only ones of us who actually visit the sick or imprisoned, or if assigning the bishop's table-concerns to a deacon sets the bishop free to be a potentate again, then the office of deacon ceases to be a gift. When we recover this office, it must be as a symbol of service for us all.

Amid these other ministries, the pastor presides. But liturgical presiding is not a matter of filling up the room with oneself. The ancient story, told in a second-century letter of Irenaeus that Eusebius preserves in his *Ecclesiastical*

History, is that when Polycarp came to Rome and was in the local Christian assembly, Anicetus, the current bishop of Rome, presided exactly by yielding place to Polycarp at the table—he made room for Polycarp to pray the thanksgiving. *Yielding place* is often the form of presiding. Keeping silence, paying attention to others, quietly caring, loving, attending to the spirit of the room—these are some of the methods of such yielding. Of course, such yielding place at the table can be an important form of ecumenical hospitality, a way to sign full communion when a visiting pastor and a visiting congregation is present. But yielding place occupies much of the ordinary ways of presiding on any Sunday: the presider yields to the readers and the leaders of prayer; the presider yields to the assisting minister; the presider—in mutual greetings and in mutual service—yields to the whole congregation. This is a participatory meeting, and the pastor's ministry is to the well-being of the whole assembly.

So we need to say this: pastors carry on an important table service. They do so in preaching, in presiding among a community enacting the sacraments, and in calling for attention to the hungry and the poor. This image of "the meal," of Christianity at the table, provides us one important source for the spirituality of the pastor.

THE PRACTICE OF TABLE SERVICE

But several other things must be said about meals and ministers.

For one thing, to use service at the table as a primary image for ministry will of course imply that our pastors are to be *servants*. Leaders, of course, have power. Leaders invested with religious-symbolic meaning have, as we have seen, extraordinary power. In Christianity, leaders must be constantly turning that power to the purposes of the assembly, to the honoring and loving and serving of each of the people, especially of the little and least ones. This assertion is not the same as saying that a pastor must always be seeking the good opinion of others, must always be currying favor with other powerful people in the congregation, for example, or must draw new power to himself or herself by the appearance of humility. No, Christian leadership has appropriate authority. We ought not fool ourselves: our leaders, our pastors, our cantors do have power. It is rather that power, in Christian use, must be continually broken, turned to service, turned toward assembly building, and turned toward love. The business of these servants is to set out the food of the gospel and to yield the importance of themselves in favor of the importance of that food and of the assembly around that food. Pastors need to occupy the paradox of this authority-that-serves.

But then, for another thing, all of the church's table servers, all of its ministers, will need themselves also to be guests, also to be served. "Insofar as I am a bishop," goes the saying attributed to Augustine, "I am in danger. Insofar as I am one of the faithful, I am safe." Bishops, pastors, presiders, and all ministers, will also sometimes need to be safe. The current practice, in some places, of the presider being served from the holy table by another communicant, receiving the bread and cup preferably last, after the others, is a good practice. It can function in our times as a clear sign of hospitality and of the goodness of the food, probably the original intention of the classic practice of the presider communing first and by his own hand. But this practice can also be an important sign today of the presider's neediness. So all the ministers come as beggars, hands out for bread, to that same table. They cannot always, always serve. Only Christ can do that, and he also serves them, in their deep need.

Furthermore, ministers who are responsible for table service in the church need to work on extending a life of hospitality into the flow of their own daily existence. Welcoming others to a gracious table, treasuring and sharing food, being with others as a good guest, thinking about and exercising appropriate limits in consumption, simplifying one's own consumption, caring about world hunger—these disciplines also belong to the practice of a table server. Also at home Paul's counsel pertains: "Welcome one another, therefore, just as Christ has welcomed you, for the glory of God" (Rom. 15:7). Of course, in a culture of seemingly unlimited abundance, all sorts of pathologies can swirl around food and its use. The Christian community is not immune from these, nor does it necessarily possess their solutions. But continued thanksgiving for the goodness of food, continued accent on the sharing of food within healthy limits, and continued devotion to the hungry of the world can help.

The very materiality of the central actions of the Christian church—human bodies together in a meeting and the shared words and songs of that meeting, the water of the foundational washing, and the food and drink of the recurrent meal—may suggest that the spirituality of the pastor, of the one who cares for the stewardship of these central things, might better be called a *carnality*. The Christian movement—at least, the part of the Christian movement that needs *pastors*, the part that has meetings and sacraments—loves and honors the flesh. Then pastors, too, are called to honor the body: their bodies and also the bodies of any and all who meet with them. Pastors are called to care about food: good food, shared food, honest food, beautiful food, the sources of food, the limits of food, those hungry for food, the earth that makes food possible. And pastors are called to care about water: local water, clean water, the sources of water, shared water. One of the ways this care can come to expression is by pastors intentionally learning the local ecologies of food and water and then helping to lead the community to care about the just connections of these ecologies to the global systems of food sharing and water health.

But the *ritual* way this care comes to expression is through *thanksgiving*. In the Eucharist, the pastor stands at the table and gives thanks, proclaiming how this food and all food comes from God, proclaiming the mystery of God now using this food to give us life through Jesus Christ, begging the Spirit of God to form us in the sharing of food. At Baptism, similarly, the pastor stands at the font and gives thanks: for water, for this water, begging the Spirit to hover over this assembly and all the world to bring life through death in Christ. Such acts of thanksgiving—such *eucharistia* at table and at font—are key signs of the vocation and spirituality of a pastor, of what a pastor *is*.

A pastor serves the table of the gospel, leads to the table through the water, gives thanks at the table, shares the food of the table.

Then, within the life of the church, the work of the pastor may rightly and essentially turn toward the accomplishment of the still-needed, table-related reforms that we have already mentioned. Here are at least some of those reforms, now rephrased as counsel to a pastor:

♦ Teach and love and lead in your congregation until the Holy Communion is the principal service of every Sunday, strongly at the heart of a fully participatory meeting.

♦ Use and teach the lectionary as a banquet of Scripture, and learn its gifts and structure.

♦ Preach so that the Word is practically edible, so that the sermon says the same thing the bread and cup say: the Spirit poured out; Jesus Christ for you; life amidst our death.

♦ Have a single reading desk in the midst of the assembly as a table of the Word.

✦ Encourage local intercessions to be made every Sunday for the urgent famines of the world.

✦ Let the table of your assembly be a strong and beautiful table, set out so that the assembly has a sense of gathering around it.

✦ Set out a loaf of real bread and a cup of good wine—or, as needed, a cup and flagon of good wine, perhaps to be shared out then in many cups—and deal with these gifts and with all of the communicants with deep reverence. Perhaps you have already worked on the recovery of the cup in your assembly, on that most beautiful and most clean of the methods of common drinking. But there is still much wafer-host use or much precut bread in our churches. It is long past time that all of us should be done with these Western medieval and then American nineteenth-century malformations, based either on the Carolingian reading of the requirement of a pure priestly bread for the "sacrifice" or simply on a supposed quick practicality. It is long past time that all of us might begin to recover the ancient and profound Christian practice of sharing an actual loaf of recognizable, local, real, beautiful bread.

✦ Make thanksgiving at the table as well as you are able. Learn and use the remarkable new treasury of the church's prayers. Take joy in this calling to give thanks at table. Learn the task and at least some of the words by heart. Then, in humility, at the end of the prayer, ask the Spirit to teach us to pray and so pray with the assembly in that prayer of Jesus for bread and forgiveness with which the church's table prayers have usually been concluded.

✦ Welcome all of the baptized to eat and drink at the table. All of them. And do not be afraid if one who is not baptized is drawn to this table of Christ. Feed them. Jesus Christ is our bathing pool himself—as well as our banquet of life. If they come, drawn to his gift, feed them. But then welcome them to come deeper and deeper into Christ through catechesis and baptism.

✦ Send the holy bread and cup to those who are absent, and do it as soon as possible, preferably as an extension of the Sunday liturgy.

✦ Make sure there is a collection for the hungry and the poor. Do not fool yourself that you are solving the world-hunger problem or finally doing justice. You are rather making a sign of the truth of God that you yourself have received in this meal. Then send or distribute the collection in a responsible and faithful way.

✦ Be sent yourself, with all the assembly, as famine relief in the world.

✦ Sing your way through this whole table-*ordo*, Sunday after Sunday.

✦ Recover the celebration of the Vigil of Easter as the great annual feast: fire and light, then all the stories, then a great occasion of baptizing, then the Eucharist.

✦ Labor for full communion between the churches, and—to the extent possible—celebrate full communion in your local community.

✦ Teach and use baptism as the way someone is introduced into this meal assembly, and let the meal assembly, its thanksgiving, and its sending to the poor remind you that you are baptized.

✦ Help those who are catechumens, those who are coming to baptism and their accompanying sponsors, learn the meal-ways of the church, including the Christian interest in feeding the hungry and the outsiders.

✦ Teach and teach that this meal practice of the church is both an economic and an ecological proposal to the world: sustainable consumption within the fragile and beautiful limits of God's good earth. This continuing reform is immensely important. Such a proposal can be lost amid the use of the Holy Supper as if it were an individually received religious consumer good, as if it were only the concern of private piety.

✦ Resist those who publicly wish to make of Christianity something else: a marketed technique for individual self-realization; a powerful, political, lobbying connection to the current Imperium; an institution that establishes the power of the religious leaders, publicly accentuates sentimental religious issues, and ignores the actual famines; or a worldwide monarchy with a single king and royal pronouncements. No. Christianity is a meal. Its leaders are table servers. Let beggars come. Then let all the political chips fall where they may. For, astonishingly, in this assembly, through these ministers, the holy Triune God is setting out the food.

✦ Finally, as you seek to do all of these things well, know you will fail. Come yourself, beggar in need, with your hands out.

So, say it this way: Christianity is a meal fellowship. And ministry is table service. There are certainly other ways it could be said. Christianity is a great washing, for example, with our meetings being a constant reimmersion in that bath. Or Christianity is a movement around a Word that does what it says. But, for thinking about what a pastor is, what a pastor does, how a pastor lives, this old image may help. A pastor serves tables.

Once, in the sacristy before an ecumenical prayer service in the Week of Prayer for Christian Unity, I was speaking with a Salvation Army captain whom I had come to know and respect. He is a man who works among the most destitute people of Philadelphia. In the course of the remarkable openness of this conversation, I suddenly felt free enough to ask, "How is it that members of the Army, for all of their care for the Scriptures, never celebrate the Lord's Supper?" He replied, saying something like this: "We trust that Christ has made us his own body and is breaking and giving us away in the world." I was, of course, stunned, wishing that I and my frequently communing co-religionists could know something of this piety. I was both deeply moved and silent, feeling a little foolish, wishing I knew what to say. But, after a pause, he was the one who continued, "You know, now and then I go off to a Lutheran or an Episcopal church to go to Holy Communion."

Ah, how we need each other, challenge each other, enable each other to live out the significance of the meeting and its faith. I found myself glad that those Lutheran or Episcopalian churches welcome him to the table. They need his witness and his life. But he also needs them. He needs the concrete reality of the gift of this meal, the presence of this sign, this gift of grace in his hand, in order to live out something of its significance.

According to the Lukan story, the pilgrims to Emmaus ran back to Jerusalem—back to the place of death—as witnesses to faith. Indeed, it is as if they themselves had become the holy bread to feed the faith of others, as if they were the "portions sent to those for whom nothing is prepared." But first they were surprised and fed themselves.

I am not a Salvation Army captain, nor am I a primitive disciple. I am a pastor, responsible for meal keeping in the church. I will hope that some of the folks at the meal will understand how the direction of the commerce of this meal exchange is all toward giving away food and mercy and help for the life of the world, how the meal itself incorporates us into this economy. I will hope that I can keep coming to understand something of this myself.

But first I too will put out my hands.

With many other people of the movie-going public in the late twentieth century, I too was enthralled with the film Babette's Feast. Drawn from the short story of the same name by Isak Dinesen, the film images the two daughters of a pietist pastor who, in spite of their parsimonious table practice, give kind hospitality to a refugee from civil war in Paris, employing her as a cook, even though they cannot afford such help. What they do not know is that this woman is one of the greatest chefs of France. Astonishingly, *this refugee woman wins the lottery and uses all of her winnings, everything she has, to give these sisters and their guests the finest meal that is possible. The meal itself is even a taste of mercy flowing everywhere, of what was lost and failed being at last restored.*

I do not think that we can simply go out and order Babette's feast. At the time of the film's release, I shared the revulsion at restaurants that made more-or-less the same menu available, at a significant price, to people who wanted to purchase the experience. I found myself thinking that it would truly be the feast only if you couldn't afford it, if someone paid all they had for it, and if it was given to you and to others. In ordinary life, I have not sat down to such a table—though, I have begun to taste this meal, I think, sometimes at the table with my wife, sometimes with my guests and with my children, sometimes as a guest myself. And, at one treasured restaurant that my wife and I visit only on extraordinary occasions, the people who serve the tables strongly remind me of the care and serving dignity exercised both by Babette and by the other simple people who helped her in the kitchen and at the table. From these people there never come those table-filling, self-focused greetings—"Hi! I'm Charlie! I'll be your server. How're we doing tonight?"—but, rather, careful, attentive, nonintrusive but still quite personal, utterly professional service. Such service is amazing to see and even more amazing to receive.

As a pastor, in the sacraments—astonishing, given-away, all-costing feast that they are—I do not want to be like that pietist pastor. Perhaps not even like his daughters, for all of their kindness. I want to be like that wait-staff.

4

The Pastor in Remembering the Poor

Diakonia

According to the Apostle Paul's own account of an important early Christian agreement in Jerusalem, the agreement that acknowledged his and Barnabas's mission among the nations, Peter, James, and John asked only one thing of these now acknowledged missionaries. It was not that they should enforce circumcision or any of the laws of purity among those Gentiles who wished to become Christians. It was not that they should continually defer to the authority of Jerusalem. It was simply that they should remember the poor. Which very thing, says Paul, "was actually what I was eager to do" (Gal. 2:10).

"Remember the poor," say Peter and James and John, those "pillars" of the church (Gal. 2:9), those human stones in God's new temple, those ancient witnesses to Christ, those old pastors. "Remember the poor," echoes Paul, the preacher, the new apostle and pastor, the one marginal to the old center. That remembrance was one basic thing they agreed upon, one root implication of the gospel they all wished to serve. Make the gospel available to everyone, and remember the poor. Our unity is found in the gospel, and there flows from that gospel, then, the admonition we give to each other to remember the poor.

What did they mean? There have been scholars who argued that "the poor" had become a technical term for the congregation of Jewish Christians in Jerusalem, a term that built upon the linguistic use of the Hebrew Scriptures, especially in the Psalms. These scholars thought that the Jerusalem community regarded itself as the *anawim*, as the faithful remnant that waited for God, together with God's own suffering Messiah. Christians did indeed believe that this Messiah spoke in the Psalms. For example, in one important passage they heard Christ saying, "From you comes my praise in the great congregation; my vows I will pay before those who fear him. The poor shall eat and be satisfied" (Ps. 22:25-26a). Furthermore, we can surmise from fragmentary evidence in later writings that there may indeed have been a Jewish-Christian group in Palestine that called itself "the poor ones," the *Ebionites*, to use their supposed title. But such evidence as we have for this group is only from the third and fourth centuries, not the first. We do know from elsewhere in his letters that Paul certainly did care for a collection for the sake of the poor among the Christians in Jerusalem (Rom. 15:25-29; 1 Cor. 16:1-3; 2 Corinthians 8–9). But it seems more likely that these were actually poverty-stricken and hungry people, the victims of famine and economic pressures, not simply bearers of a religiously symbolic name. It seems more likely that Paul believed that God's promise of food, found repeatedly in the Scriptures and celebrated especially in that psalm so important to the Christian account of Christ's passion and death—Psalm 22—was given to all the poor of the world. It seems more likely that Peter, James, John, and Paul all meant what they said, in the plain significance of the words.

"Remembering" thus includes the idea of taking a collection and sending it to those who need it. "Remembering" is not just a mental undertaking by individuals. Something actually happens. The very "apostle to the Gentiles" works to enable and even to transport to a place of need (Rom. 15:28) the real gifts that belong to a new economy of mutual support. We have seen that such a collection survived as a liturgical practice in second-century Rome, as a direct consequence, a necessary entailment, of the centrality of the community's meal, the Lord's Supper. Furthermore, we have reflected on care for such a collection and its sending as one of the three identifying tasks of the pastor, exploring some of the outlines of this care as these are inevitably interwoven with the faithful exercise of the preaching task and the table-serving task. In that sense, we have already considered *diakonia*.

But "remember" also seems to carry a surplus of meaning. Those who hear the gospel know themselves in need, know themselves served by the one who became poor for their sake (2 Cor. 8:9). They may then come to know themselves addressed by all the unconsoled trauma his cross reveals in the world, and thus know themselves identified with all who are poor, all with whom he identifies. To trust in the gospel is to have one's view of the world changed. Indeed, "remember

Jesus Christ" (2 Tim. 2:8) is never far away from "remember the poor." Those who share what they have to add to the community's collection, then, ought not so much do so out of the status that comes with wealth—even when they have it—as out of their own sense of standing in and sharing both the gospel and the aching need of the world. So Paul writes of the Macedonians that "during a severe ordeal of affliction, their abundant joy and their extreme poverty have overflowed in a wealth of generosity on their part" (2 Cor. 8:2).

The Apostle Paul preaches the gospel and remembers the poor. Something like the same vocation, albeit worked out with different, local, congregational responsibilities, belongs to the pastors of the church. It is clear that we have more to think about as we consider the significance of *diakonia* and the surplus meaning of this "remember" for the spirituality of the pastor.

THE PASTOR AND POLITICAL IMAGINATION

For one thing, we have to think about politics. The fairly common idea that Christianity should be apolitical and its leaders politically uninvolved runs significant dangers. It seems to propose that Christianity is only about another world, a spiritual world or a private world, and that Christian faith has no particular implications for the organization of concrete, public, social life. In fact, *politics* refers to the organization of the *polis*, of the city or of current public life. It does not mean simply the work of political parties or the campaigns of political candidates. And Christian faith does indeed care about the organization of our cities and our common life. Of course, Christians and their leaders must be careful that they do not claim divine sanction for matters from their own specific and frequently self-interested political agendas. Of course, Christians and their leaders need to work together with all people of good will in caring for justice and for peace, for the well-being of the earth and for social wholeness. Of course, Christians and their leaders need to acknowledge that many of the best political ideas may come from people who do not share in Christian faith. Christians believe that this is God's world—not the church's—and all of its inhabitants are gifted with the means to care for it in common.

But there are biblical and Christian ideas, ideas that Christians believe come from God, that do constantly invite us to a larger political imagination. There are proposals, arising from the center of the gospel, that do challenge every political proposal. These ideas include the assertion that this is God's beloved world and we are to remember the poor.

When, in 1519, Martin Luther wrote of the practice of the mass, he urged communicants to understand that meal as an amazing exchange, the very "commerce" of the city of God. In the Holy Communion, Christ and all of his holy ones take our wretchedness and, in exchange, give us their blessedness. In turn, we are to direct ourselves toward our neighbors in need, continuing the exchange. God does not need what we have to give. Our neighbors do. He continued:

> When you have partaken of this sacrament, therefore, or desire to partake of it, you must in turn share the misfortunes of the fellowship, as has been said.…Here your heart must go out in love and learn that this is a sacrament of love. As love and support are given to you, you in turn must render love and support to Christ in his needy ones. You must feel with sorrow all the dishonor done to Christ in his holy Word, all the misery of Christendom, all the unjust suffering of the innocent, with which the world is everywhere filled to overflowing. You must fight, work, pray, and—if you cannot do more—have heartfelt sympathy. ("The Blessed Sacrament of the Holy and True Body of Christ, and the Brotherhoods," 9)

Such a practice may constitute a spirituality for communicants, including pastors. We may even call such practice, paradoxically, a communion *carnality*, an intentional immersion in the goodness and the need of the conditions of the flesh. Such a practice is a "remembering the poor" that flows from the eucharistic "remembering Jesus Christ." But pastors surely need to teach this idea in the congregation. And they need to preside over the communal sending to its enactment.

Taking a collection and seeing to it that this collection is distributed where it will genuinely help is one form of response to "you must fight, work, pray." Indeed, such a collection is a political act. The collection will not solve the massive needs of the wretched. But by interrupting the usual flow of our economics, by bearing witness to need, the collection can also bear witness to God's merciful intention for the beloved world. The collection can poke a small hole in politics as usual. Together with their congregations and synods and larger church organizations, pastors certainly need to inquire about the responsible use of this money. Is the benevolence money, the money sent for wider church use, used well? Does it support important witness and service in the world? Are the social-service agencies with which food and money are shared addressing real problems carefully, realistically, mercifully, with minimum overhead and with funds mostly flowing to people genuinely in need? Furthermore, pastors will need to care about this collection in the political conversation of the local church. Church councils and treasurers, by vocation, rightly care about responsibly paying the local bills, responsibly protecting the health of the congregation's property, programs, and fiscal reputation, responsibly paying salaries and benefits. It is to be hoped that such leaders also catch the vision of wider need and wider responsibility. But since pastors come from "away from here" and are themselves signs of the wider linkage of the congregations that call them, and since they have something like the apostolic commission to preach the gospel, it is also true that they, *by vocation*, call the congregation to "fight, work, pray" beyond the local concerns. Pastors, like Paul, rightly call an assembly to benevolence, to money and food sent away from here to others than "our own." Pastors rightly urge us all to see that collection as a sign of political imagination.

But it is not the only sign of political imagination. Also in the Christian community, it is true that "charity" can function to salve the wounded conscience of the sensitive while doing little to actually help and leaving a wretched social situation essentially unchanged. "Remember the poor" does not only mean the collection. It also calls the Christian to inhabit, at least with his or her imagination, something of the affliction of our neighbors and of the trauma of the world. From such inhabiting will arise political action: "you must fight, work, pray." It is not only the collection that is sent at the end of the liturgy. It is the assembly itself.

Pastors, of course, are among the sent. They, too, will join with all the others in working out ways to bring to expression in common life the things we have seen in the assembly—about God and the world and our neighbors. They will try to act justly and peaceably with their neighbors, seeking reconciliation when they do not. They will seek volunteer opportunities, perhaps planned by the Christian community itself, perhaps found in the neighborhood. They will engage in political debate and political action. They will seek to know more about social change, about situations of human need and injustice, about the local and global networks of food exchange, about the environment, about the other living species and their well-being. They will work to balance the sometimes competing concerns of justice and ecology, remembering that the poorest people are often both those first hurt by a degraded economy and those worst hurt by a degraded environment. They will listen respectfully to the political proposals of the leaders of their own and other countries, weighing out the truth, but also suspecting the potent, distorting force of untempered self-interest and uncriticized power. They will be especially, vigorously suspicious of reasons given for war: from a Christian point of view it is extremely difficult to establish the necessity of a just war. Sometimes, in the face of war or of yet other systemic injustices, they will engage in protest and the remarkable sign of nonviolent public engagement, humbly but boldly, begging God for forgiveness if they are wrong. And sometimes—rarely, almost never, and only when accompanied by public accountability and by all the protections of the innocent that are possible—they may even have to act violently or ask others to act violently in their name, as soldiers or police or even simply as citizens, especially when the lives of the unprotected weak are involved and when all else has failed. In all of this, pastors will simply be Christians and citizens among other Christians and other citizens. They will have no privileged place. This engagement is simply what Christians should do in God's good earth. "Remember the poor," say Paul and Peter and the liturgy of Christians.

There is no specific political program, no uncriticized ideology, no privileged political party implied by this Christian political engagement. Rather, Paul's "remember the poor" and Luther's "fight, work, pray for the wretched" are expressions of a political imagination that begins with faith in the triune God—in the God who made and loves all things, in Jesus Christ who shares the lot of the most wretched, in the Spirit hovering with healing over all the world. Such an imagination pokes holes in every ideology, destabilizes any self-assured program. God is God, and we are to remember the poor. Of course, we will use political parties and ideologies and programs, weighing which are best to aid in the social care for the earth. But we will not believe in them. And we will try to resist being used by them, as arms of governmental power or of political maneuvering.

Still, such political action for systemic change should never lead us to despair of the importance of the collection nor to abandon the protest involved in a simple act of charity. Of course, almsgiving and the communal collection often arise from mixed motives, are never quite enough, but they nonetheless do witness to a God who cares for actual, individual lives. "Remember the poor," we hear echoed again.

But, in the care for this political imagination, there are several specific matters that do fall, by vocation, to the pastor. The most important is the well-being of the assembly's liturgy, its communal practice of Word and Sacrament, the source of our vision of a world held in grace. In a certain sense, Sunday after Sunday, that assembly itself—when it is clearly gathered around the gospel—is our basic political act, our basic protest about the organization of the *polis*, our root encounter with God's good earth and God's presence with the wretched, our root sending. But then, in addition, as we have seen, the pastor sees to it that there is a collection, that the collection is responsibly distributed, and that there is a further sending of us all, away from here, to those not included here and to the care of the earth itself. Furthermore, the pastor has a special calling to teach this political and environmental significance of the assembly's liturgy. And the pastor bears a responsibility to counter the tendency to turn the assembly's political imagination into ideology. The needy of the world include the most wretched and the most poor, but they also include the rich and the powerful, as the biblical story of Naaman the leper (2 Kings 5; Luke 4:27) makes clear. Political opponents must not be made into enemies. Nor may we understand ourselves as the savior. Christians need to learn, over and over, that the sorting of people belongs to the angels at the final judgment, not to the church now (Matt. 13:49). Grace is everywhere and for all, not just for us, but also for us. This paradox—serious political action yet active imagination of and compassion for the situation of those who disagree—is yet another paradox the pastor is invited to inhabit and to teach.

THE SEASONS OF POVERTY

The vocation of the pastor in the remembrance of the poor can find significant help in the flow of the liturgical year. Every season of that year may, in its own way, help with the clear proclamation of the gospel, the celebration of the grace of God for all the earth, the well-being of the Sunday assembly and the urgency of the sending. But especially Advent and Lent recall the church's awareness of the situation of the poor.

Advent tries to tell the truth about the need of the world. As the world grows darker—at least in the northern hemisphere—the readings and the hymnody of the Christian assembly, its simplicity, and the slowly growing light of its wreath of candles all speak of waiting and hoping. The point is not a pretended waiting, as if Jesus were not yet born and we were waiting for his coming. That use of Advent inevitably short-circuits its elemental power. Rather, Advent helps the church tell the truth about the actual conditions of the current world—in winter in the northern hemisphere, but through the imagery of that concrete situation also in all the world in all of our seasons. The darkness may be a symbol of waiting for the light, just as hungry people wait for food in all seasons, war-devastated countries wait for peace, prisoners wait for release, the poor wait for the possibility of hope. The dark time of year is taken by the church to stand for a world waiting for the dominion of God and the biblical stories of such waiting become the stories of our lectionary.

At the same time, the church celebrates the very presence of God's mercy in the midst of situations of need. The new/old color of Advent, used in the church for paraments and vestments, may be deep blue, the color of night just before dawn. In any case, those candles do continue to burn, widening their circle on the wreath. "One, two, three, four," we count. And every Sunday is just that: *Sunday*, the feast of Light, the feast of the Resurrection. The Gospels tell of Jesus Christ come among our need and all the way into our death, already giving the down payment on the dominion of God, being himself the light in the darkness and the source of the life-giving Spirit. The stories of John the Baptist preaching and Mary conceiving, of Jesus reinterpreting the old ideas of the end of the world, of the child in the poverty of the manger all echo what Christian faith trusts is the deepest intention of God: life from death; something from nothing; hope in impossibility; justification for the ungodly. These Advent stories are then all told at the Eucharist—the meal that proclaims the basic story of life springing from death and plenty where we might only find poverty. These stories and that meal set us free to pay the clearer attention to the actual situations of acute poverty and endless waiting with which the world is filled.

We need Advent. We need its truth, its simplicity, its honesty about poverty and waiting, its gospel of God's mercy dwelling in and transfiguring our darkness. Pastors are right to defend Advent, making its themes available to their people, resisting its abandonment in a culture of instant gratification and excessive consumerism. If Advent is taken seriously, it will not allow us to forget the poor. Of course, we will not be much helped by scolding. We will not be particularly helped by pastors who yell at us because there are December parties (although surely, in the church itself, a "Christmas party" will be scheduled during the twelve days of Christmas, not during Advent, as part of the gift the church has to give us all). Still, parties in the dark time have their own bittersweet reality, their own longing for something the parties will never reach. We need pastors who will tell us clearly, boldly, gently, truthfully something of what that is: "Remember the poor" and "Remember Jesus Christ."

We also need pastors who make Advent spirituality a basic component of their own spiritual life throughout the year. Here is yet another paradox in which pastors may dwell: While we live in the light, rejoice in the light, sing of the light, darkness can be beautiful in any time of year. It calls us to rest and to hope, inviting us to acknowledge our inabilities and our fears. It stills our work and even our sense that we can do it, making us all poor, bringing us to seek out sheltering community. In the darkness everybody is in need, and those who know what the darkness reveals will not be surprised by the discovery of the abyss of need in each of the people they encounter. Pastors may rightly be lovers of the darkness, remembering the poor but also remembering the promise of the God who identifies with the poor, the feast that has begun like a fountain springing up in the desert, the real though hidden joy. Also in the bright times of year these aching and as yet unanswered needs continue, as does this surprising mercy. *Advent spirituality*—that may provide one current way that a contemporary pastor may live out something of George Herbert's counsel: "The country Parson is generally sad...nevertheless, he sometimes refresheth himself, as knowing that nature will not bear everlasting droopings..."

The other season of the church that reinforces the Pauline call to remember the poor is Lent. Of course, Lent is baptismal time. That is, it was originally the old church's period in which candidates for baptism were finally prepared. Then, when it became the forty days prior to the annual paschal or Easter feast, the greatest occasion of baptism in the life of the church, it also was used to call all of the church to baptismal renewal, to invite us all again to walk in the mercy washed over us in baptism. The renewals of recent years have restored this idea among us. Our lectionary helps us to come up to the Easter feast once again—together with all those who are coming to baptism—as if we were the woman at the well being offered the living water in our local font (so Lent 3 A), as if we were the man born blind coming again through that water to see (so Lent 4 A). And at the very start of Lent, in the Gospel of Ash Wednesday, we are invited to a Christian practice of the disciplines of Lent: fasting, prayer, and almsgiving. Also here we hear, "remember the poor."

The point of Christian fasting in Lent should not be to demonstrate our supposedly spiritual athleticism, our gnostic ability to rise above mere flesh and its needs, as if that were any virtue. Exactly the contrary. The deepest biblical conception of fasting is that it demonstrates our own need in concert with our neighbors, with others who are wretched and hungry, with a whole world in need, as if the fast were an enacted prayer to God. Fasting is about not hiding from "your own flesh" (Isa. 58:7) in both senses: our relatives—all the others who share mortal existence with us—and our bodily selves, in own fleshly existence as well. *Not hiding from mortality*, telling the truth—those are the outlines of the discipline. And such a discipline may come to expression best by fasting from pretense, from self-righteousness, from misuse of the earth, and from acts of injustice as well as from self-indulgence.

In any case, classic Christian fasting is conjoined with intercessory prayer for a world in need and with almsgiving—with the sharing of the food and money we are *not* consuming ourselves—as a sign of the solidarity of our life with those whose lives of poverty are their only prayer. One of the Prayers of the Day appointed for Ash Wednesday reads as follows:

> Merciful God,
> accompany our journey through these forty days.
> Renew us by our baptism
> to provide for those who are poor,
> to pray for those in need,
> and to fast from self-indulgence,
> that we may find our treasure in the life of your Son,
> Jesus Christ, our Savior and Lord...

"Our treasure in the life of your Son"—this profound reinterpretation of the "treasure in heaven" from the passage of the Sermon on the Mount that is used as the Gospel for Ash Wednesday, invites us then to see where "heaven" really is. It invites us to stand with all those with whom Christ stands. As the Lenten days proceed, stories of the passion and cross of Jesus are also told, but they are told exactly to insert us again in the gospel of the God who comes with life-giving and surprising mercy among the wretched of the world. It is this gospel into which we have been baptized. The disciplines of Lent belong to God's gift of baptismal meaning, being lived out in our daily lives. "Remember Jesus Christ" goes intimately linked with "remember the poor," especially in Lent, especially in baptism.

But, in a cultural moment marked by excessive consumption and by widespread justification of the priority of the search for the well-being of the self, these disciplines also need to be taught. Again, what we need is not scolding and certainly not self-righteousness from the religiously observant. Rather, we need pastors who love the people they serve and love the gospel of the life-giving mercy of God come among the poor. We need pastors who themselves try to reimagine Lent, its baptismal centrality and its urgent disciplines, and who teach clearly the death that is resident in self-centered consumption and the joyful life that abounds in God's merciful gift to us all in common. Lent is another time of telling the truth about our need. Because of that truth, Lent may provide a further annual support for the importance of the Sunday collection, the importance of the Sunday sending, and the importance of the Christian political imagination.

Still, neither Advent not Lent should be regarded as grim. There is deep joy hidden in the darkness of Advent. And in Lent, at least on every Sunday, Easter itself runs out to greet us, embracing us and clothing us with the resurrection even before we get there, like the prodigal son being welcomed by the father who races out to meet him even before he can repent. The truth about a needy world, when it is conjoined with the gospel of the triune God, is a joyful, festive truth. Advent as a bright darkness, Lent as a joyful fast belong to the spirituality of the pastor, to the wonderful paradoxes in which she or he may walk.

THE POOR IN SPIRIT

But another kind of poverty also explicitly confronts the pastor. Engaged in what seems like a mundane conversation, suddenly the pastor realizes that the other person is speaking, achingly, of the emptiness in life—or the fear or the loneliness or the sorrow. Or the sin. A man begins to talk about the uncontrollable and violent rage he sometimes knows. A woman, weeping, starts to talk of the child she abandoned years ago. The stories are endless, agonizing. A pastor—at least a pastor who will listen, who seems to have something to do with God, and who makes herself or himself available—will inevitably hear these stories. Such a pastor will also know, when he or she looks at any gathering of people, including especially the Sunday assembly this pastor serves, that the room is filled with such stories. These people are also the poor, the wretched whose lives are an abyss of need, the violated and the violating, living creatures in need of God.

One must be careful not to use the idea of poverty only in this spiritualized sense. The gospel of the triune God entails a concern for the actual economics of household earth, the actual state of the physically hungry. We eat a real meal in Christianity and we are sent with real food to our neighbors. Furthermore, if the Christianity of the Northern and Western world turns its sense of justice, reconciliation, and love only toward the interior needs of its own people, it will rightly be accused of uncritically adopting the psychological orientation of Western culture and calling that adoption "the gospel."

At the same time, interiorly agonized, mourning, and guilt-ridden people are not a new and only Western phenomenon. Neither is a godly cure of souls. And current psychological insight can be a rich gift in such care. No, these people—also in biblical perspective (think of the voice of the psalmist!)—are among the wretched poor. These people are also *us*. These are our stories. We are, together, these sinners. These are also the poor among whom God comes in mercy, light in the darkness, life amidst death. And the *diakonia* of the assembly and of its pastor needs also to be turned toward them: toward the mourning, the sorrowful, the lonely, the despairing, and toward the sinner in need of forgiveness and new life.

This book is not the place to sketch a thoroughgoing theory of pastoral care. We need here only to note that a pastor who understands his or her spirituality from the presiding tasks of the liturgy will see that pastoral care unfolds from these liturgical tasks. To preach a meaningful sermon, telling the truth about real human sin, need, and death, and about God's act of grace in Christ, will open doors to personal conversations. To proclaim the forgiveness of sins communally and publicly in the assembly will lead to occasions when the forgiveness of sins needs to be proclaimed particularly and privately. To articulate what church is as it gathers around Baptism, Word, and Eucharist and to send that assembly in mission will give occasion, personally and privately, to proclaim that mercy of God that can reconcile an alienated person to the identity and mission of the church. To be genuinely trustworthy in the assembly will rightly lead to people trusting you with their agony, with their stories, with what they need to say.

And, dear pastor, just as at the liturgy, you need to continue to be trustworthy, also personally, also in that private conversation.

Such trustworthiness will include your own willingness to be available but also your own knowledge of your limits. Someone who seeks you out in his or her distress comes to you only partly because of what he or she sees in—or projects onto—you and your personality. Such a person comes also in search of God, of a word from God, a sign from God. You are a pastor and you know yourself, critically, as a symbol. You need to be there, fully engaged. Paradoxically, you also need to be interiorly withdrawn, yourself before God, making safe space for the other, commending her or him to God, critically aware of and controlling your own counter-transference, the needs you are seeking to have met through your *own* projections. Your knowledge of your limits will also be enacted by learning as much as you can about wise pastoral care, by working on your skill at referral when the problem includes dimensions much too large for you, by giving what you genuinely do have in catechesis and in the word of forgiveness, and by not being always available. You are not God. You do need to rest. It is not a mature gift to the other to seem as if you are always available.

But, when you are available, your service to the other will be especially clear if it is about your giving those gifts you genuinely do have to give. A pastor who presides in the midst of the communal exercise of the Word of God and the holy sacraments, has especially these very things to give particularly, personally, privately—but in the name of the full assembly and in communion with it—to people in need. It may be that a pastor will perceive that what is needed here is a gracious and honest form of teaching—*catechesis*—or a clear and open conversation about what in the world these ideas of the faith could really mean—*apologetics*, it might be called. It may be that talking for a while beside the font can help this person recover a sense of baptismal vocation. But it may be that wise referral to another—a counselor or another teacher—is what is needed. This Christian business, after all—the business both enacted and symbolized by the assembly—is a mature, communal business. It ought not be exercised only in the formation of individual loyalties. In any case, your availability will need to mean the same reliability in personal encounter that is so clearly symbolized in the assembly. You will need to exercise your own utter confidentiality with what is told you, your sense of carrying these communications as if you were carrying the mystery of the other with deep respect, like you were standing with them at the Holy Communion. Still, here too, you will bear communal responsibility, urging the other toward wider communication when it is needed, suggesting paths toward healing and reparation with others who have been hurt, and not agreeing to collaborate in keeping violent crime against others as a secret when it needs to be set out in the open light. Confidentiality and communal responsibility make up another paradoxical pair that a pastor negotiates.

But pastors should be especially skilled in sensing that what is needed is, in fact, straightforward *absolution*. Not circuitous speeches; not excuses, but the authority of direct forgiveness, in the name of God. Pastors should know how to see that a conversation is becoming a confession. Or they should know what to do when someone asks to make a confession. They should know the materials of their own ritual books and the possibility of making ritual use of the community's gathering space or the community's font, also for this particular announcement of the gospel. Of course, pastors should know that the presenting sin, the first thing named, may not be a sin at all or may not be what the other really wants or needs to talk about. They should be prepared to receive what is said respectfully, to make gentle inquiries, and to wait patiently. And they should know that they themselves are sinners. This knowledge should never lead to turning such a pastoral conversation into an occasion in which the visitor is taking care of the pastor. But classic forms of private confession had a fine way, nonetheless, to bring this truth to expression: at the very end of the ritual, the pastor says, as the visitor is leaving, "And pray for me, a sinner." That is all.

This *diakonia* of the pastor also flows out of the liturgy. Critical of yourself as a symbol, you nonetheless exercise that symbolic leadership in the assembly, turning its power to support a community around God's mercy in Word and Sacrament. Aware of your limitations, knowing yourself to be a sinner with your own stories of sorrow, you nonetheless hear confessions or stand with persons in grief, genuinely seeking understanding side by side with them, refusing to be the judge yourself, announcing in the triune name the one thing you have a word for, even when you do not understand it—*forgiveness*. Knowing yourself to be baptized into Christ, you assist the congregation—communally and personally—to remember those who belong to him, to remember the poor.

When I was a little boy in Sunday school, we used to sing a common, pious song. "Come into my heart, come into my heart, come into my heart, Lord Jesus," it went. "Come in today, come in to stay, come into my heart, Lord Jesus." Years later, when I was in seminary, I recalled that song again. The president of our seminary, himself at least partly molded in the traditions of Lutheran pietism, was a fine preacher, with a remarkable sense for the gospel and a great care for his hearers. But the sermon I most remember included these lines: "When you sing 'Come into my heart, Lord Jesus,' be assured. He will come. But he will bring with him—into you heart and into your life—all those who belong to him: all the little ones; all the wretched; all the poor. If you pray alone in your closet, it will suddenly be full."

About the same time, in seminary, I heard the famous, post–World War II German Lutheran bishop, Hans Lilje, speak. He too said something that sticks in my memory to this day. He was praising a deaconess with the best praise he could find. He said, "She knew herself so well, she understood so deeply her own need of God and her own sin, that she was never shocked by anything she ever encountered in someone else. Never shocked."

And then, not long after, I read the poem of George Herbert, called simply "Sion" and included in his book of poetry, The Temple, a book filled with images drawn from the liturgy. The poem celebrates the beauty of Solomon's ancient temple, its architecture and its great bronze pool—evoking thereby Christian liturgical practice, even as the whole book makes Christian liturgy to be something like that temple—but then occur these lines, addressed to God:

> *All Solomon's sea of brass and world of stone*
> *Is not so dear to thee as one good groan.*

These lines ought not be misunderstood. Herbert loved the liturgy, rejoiced in the beauty of its words, actions, and patterns. But, paradoxically, that very beloved liturgy yielded to something else more important: groans.

Those three words have kept after me, kept working on making me a pastor, kept saying to me something like "remember the poor."

"One good groan." My groans, too. But not only mine.

"Never shocked. Never." Is that true?

"He will come—together with all those who belong to him." Remember Jesus Christ. Remember the poor.

PART TWO

Living from the Liturgy
A Little Catechism for the Pastor

5

The Pastor in Study and Prayer

The Creed

The pastor presides in the midst of the liturgy, leading an assembly that has gathered around the Word and the sacraments. But she or he is also invited to live from that liturgy, like every other Christian believer. The surprising, life-giving grace celebrated there is also for the pastor, also for the hope, renewal, and reorientation of the pastor's life. "And also with you," declares the congregation, communally proclaiming that the presence of God and of the gospel are also for their pastor.

We have considered how one part of the baptismal inheritance, one of the catechumenal texts—the Lord's Prayer—can function as a symbol of the liturgy and of the pastor's calling to learn that liturgy and its leadership tasks by heart. Rehearsing that symbol, reflecting on its meaning, standing with the needy people to whom it gives a voice and standing before the merciful, triune God it brings to expression, living out of the surprises of bread and forgiveness—these continually renewed undertakings belong to the lifelong catechumenate of the pastor.

But there needs to be more to the pastor's life than liturgical leadership. The pastor ought not be only a symbol-person for a Christian assembly, even if the symbol is well broken. Also for the pastor there is family and communal life, and there are social and political responsibilities. Also for the pastor there needs to be delight in new knowledge, skill at making and keeping friends, attention to learning the world, facility at marking each morning and each evening, and competence in keeping the feasts. Through it all, there needs to be forgiving and being forgiven. There will be sickness and health. And, finally, there will be death.

In each person's life, all of these things may be characterized by such pungent individuality, such uniqueness, that they can be hard to describe in a general way, applicable to all of us. Perhaps little help is to be found in trying to write about how *pastors* live, learn, love, and die, as contrasted with how any Christian does these things. "Pastor" is a name for a person who presides in the assembly and carries away some of the assembly's gifts to those who are absent. It is not the primary name for a spouse or a parent or a friend or a student or a partygoer—or for the person who is dying in that bed—even when that person is also a pastor. All pastors do not look alike as they engage in these relationships, patterns, responsibilities, even though, as Christians, the mercy and grace they have known in the assembly around the gospel will be shaping their responses.

Nonetheless, the actual liturgical tasks of pastors—the tasks that have been learned by heart—will flow into these things, subtly interacting with the parenting and the politics and the festival keeping. At the same time, Christian assemblies do need presiders who keep learning about the world, keep caring about spouses and friends, and struggle to be honest about dying. A pastor's life ought not be carved up into hermetically sealed compartments. Even though there is indeed a treasured individuality in the way people live, a spirituality for pastors must also address several issues of living, learning, praying, and dying, several ways in which pastors may particularly live from the liturgy as they engage these things.

We have considered the Lord's Prayer. But the catechism—the summary symbols of the baptismal inheritance—is bigger yet. The baptismal process has brought us all, in one way or another, one time or another, through the questions of lifestyle change, through learning the content of the faith and learning how to pray with the community, to the water and the table, and so to our vocation as Christians and to the continued trust in God's forgiveness. As symbols of these, the Ten Commandments, the Creed, the Lord's Prayer, and the words of Baptism, the Supper, and the Office of the Keys belong to us all. Also to the pastor. These words are available to be rehearsed again and again, in a lifelong catechumenate. Also by the pastor.

Remember: *catechism*, here, means those symbolic texts, not some further process of question followed by right answer. Indeed, the symbols themselves are far larger than any particular questions and answers, just as they are far larger than the reflections of this book.

But if, in this baptism-centered pastoral spirituality, we have taken the Lord's Prayer to call pastors to the resonances and heart-learning of their liturgical tasks, how shall we take these other texts? Here is one idea: Let the Creed invite pastors again to study and prayer, the Ten Words (as they are called in Hebrew) center a reflection on the surprises and reorientations of a pastor's life, and the words of Baptism, the Supper, and the Keys help to prepare also a pastor for death, speaking the life-giving gospel. These texts can be used in many other ways. But, anchored in baptism and given, in this case, to people who are living out their baptismal vocation as pastors, the words can be used to frame more fully a spirituality for those pastors. What follows in the rest of this book is thus a little catechism for pastors, a small set of reflections on the relationships that may be seen between the baptismal gifts, the vocation to communal presidency in Word and Sacrament, and the exigencies of ordinary life, beginning with two matters of some consequence in the life of a pastor: *study* and *prayer*.

But how does the Creed relate to study and prayer? For that matter, what shall we make of the Creed at all?

A SYMBOL OF FAITH

The Creed may not always be taken as a gift. Sometimes, it rather seems to be understood as a test, a brief examination to see whether or not you fit with the group reciting it. It can seem like a *shibboleth* (see Judges 12:6), used to sort out the believers from the unbelievers. Indeed, the Nicene Creed may have come into use in the Sunday liturgy of the Eucharist with something like that very intention. At least, the hope seems to have been that a creed-using community of Christian believers would have been declaring that their eucharistic celebration was intended to proclaim and strengthen *orthodox* rather than heterodox faith. Current liturgical commentators frequently remark that this work might be better done by responsible preaching and by such recitation of the great works of God as can fill a fine eucharistic prayer. Indeed, some current rubrics rightly treat the Creed as an optional part of the Sunday *ordo*.

Nonetheless, it should be noted that the current Sunday use of the Nicene Creed invites us to confess together, communally, that "We believe ..." The Creed ought not be dealt with as an individual examination. It ought rather be seen as an assembly-based confession of the faith of the church, an historic text used willingly now, in communion with the ancient catholic churches, but also clearly juxtaposed to other powerful ways of articulating that same faith of the church: preaching, hymn singing, interceding, giving thanks at the table, putting our hands out for communion, and being sent to remember the poor. That any individual Christian might not quite put the matter today in the same way as the Creed does—in that fourth-century, Greek-influenced rhetoric—matters far less than that the community itself sets out these rich symbols of Christian faith in a multilayered way, intending to form us all into a multilayered faith.

But the Creed of the Western catechism is not, in the first place, the Nicene Creed but the so-called Apostles' Creed. That text summarizes in a simpler way the classic questions and responses of baptism. While this Creed, too, may be used on a Sunday, its primary home is the preparation for baptism—in which it is given as a gift to those who are coming to the water—and in the baptismal rite itself. Then, in the lifelong catechumenate of any Christian, this Creed may function as a symbol of that baptismal faith, a symbol side by side with those other symbols of baptism—texts and water and bread and wine—to recall us all to the faith into which we were grafted, as into a living tree, when we were baptized.

Symbols of the faith: that is what the creeds of the church have been called classically, just as the Lutheran confessional writings are called the "symbolical books of the Lutheran confession." A creed is a *symbol*, a gathering place for communal encounter with larger meaning, a multivalent place where many people come together, participating through the symbol in that to which it refers. Such a "meeting place" allows for diversity and difference. That is what symbols do. But then what larger meaning do we encounter in the Creed? Say it this way, for now, as one way: the Christian church teaches us to trust that God is creator of this actual, material world; God has made and still cares for all that is. In a world that largely thinks of spiritual truths as being unconnected with the material, inviting us out of here, that confession is already an astonishing assertion, a daring trust. But there is more. Far from God being distant from a world full of suffering, in this same church I am invited to trust Jesus Christ. The church teaches us to trust with our lives that God, in Christ, has shared our human life, sorrows and death, saving all things and all of us together for forgiveness and life. I am invited to trust that God's own heart, God's very own self, who God actually *is*, is encountered in the man Jesus, and that because of the resurrection we may indeed so encounter this Jesus Christ here in the meeting of the church as well as in all of those suffering ones with whom he identifies. But there is yet more. The assembly of the church itself, as it stands before the creator of all in company with the words and signs of this Jesus, believes it is enlivened by the very presence of God, called the Holy Spirit. Only so, may we come to the astonishing trust called *faith*. Yet, having said all of that, it is important to add that there are not three gods, but one God. Indeed, for Christians, this account of the Spirit enlivening the meeting so that, in a suffering world, we may gather with the Risen One before the face of the Source of all things—this trinitarian account—is what makes the trust in one God possible at all. When I was baptized I was gathered into a community that trusts these things: the actual world is good and held by God; this same God engages with the real suffering, sin, and death of all this world, and may be encountered where we had not expected God to be; and this same God gives us the gift to live out of such faith rather than out of fear and guilt and death. I was brought through the waters to trust that there is a good creation, that I can tell the truth about suffering and death, and that God's Spirit is life giving.

For Lutherans and other Christians, Luther's sixteenth-century explanations of the catechism have enabled the third- and fourth-century language of the creeds to continue to speak meaningfully. Luther's existential reinterpretations of the words, his interest in the event of God's acting, and his interest in the material and fleshly consequences and personal engagements that follow—God has created me and all that is; Jesus Christ has saved me; and I cannot believe without the Spirit—these all have helped many Christians since the sixteenth century deal with the creeds again as lively symbols.

But the work is not done. The classic Christian faith needs to be continually set out—now in our time—in new explanations, in new catechesis and apologetics, in new hymnody and preaching, and in the continued layering of symbols. Now we need to speak of the *us* as well as the *me*. Now we need to talk about faith in God amid the broken ecology of the environment and the recent flood of societal sins—war and genocide and poverty ignored. Now we need to insist on eternal life and salvation as flesh-affirming, this-worldly gifts. Now we need to rejoice in the idea of *creation* as thoroughly in harmony with intelligent, self-critical science, as encouraging our participation in the care of the earth, and as inviting us away from the delusions and dangers of a supposedly spiritual escape from the material world. The Creed does not call pastors to be legalistic and fundamentalist defenders of the literal language of the fourth century. It does call pastors to attend honestly to their own questions and yet, also, to interpret the historic faith responsibly, in company with the whole church of the ages, so that the urgently needed gift that the creeds still symbolize may be seen and received also in our time. Indeed, the *symbolic* character of the creeds also calls the pastor to juxtapose them, in the liturgy of the church, to the strong symbols of vigorous and truthful preaching, beautiful prayer, enlarged sacramental practice, and meaningful sending to service and witness and solidarity with the suffering. Seriousness about the Creed does not condone pastoral indolence.

The Creed can be seen as calling the pastor to two further things. If its first two articles confess the goodness of God's world and the seriousness of God's engagement with evil—creation and redemption, to use the theological categories—then among other things, the lifelong catechumenate of the pastor, responding to these articles, can be seen to include important *study*, important engagement with what is *so* in the world and, at the same time, important engagement with the disciplines of theology itself. And if the Third Article of the Creed confesses our need of a common life in the Spirit, then the lifelong catechumenate of the pastor can be seen to include *prayer* in that same Spirit, prayer in and with the church.

STUDY THAT DELIGHTS IN WHAT IS

Study belongs to the life of a pastor. For other Christians the baptismal gift of creation-faith may be lived out in many, many other ways. The sense of the goodness of work and rest, of family and communal life, of food and festival flows into all Christian lives from this confession. At the present time, for all of us—including pastors—a Christian life formed by the First Article of the Creed needs to include an especially deep care for the well-being of the environment. But specifically for a pastor, that baptismal gift of creation faith needs to imply a wide-ranging and lively *study*. This assertion is partly true, of course, because the tasks of a pastor in preaching and teaching call for a wise mind, skilled in the use of language and metaphor, capable of imaging the situations of others different than herself or himself, able to engage in self-criticism and in holding more than one idea together at once, interested in the lives and situations of others, fascinated by the world itself, capable of learned and generous tolerance as well as fierce and passionate defense of important ideas. Pastors owe it to their congregations, as a moral obligation of their vocation, to be persons of study.

But there is more to say. In Christian communities, the leaders—the pastors— need to be literate. They need to be able to read, not least because the Bible stands at the heart of the assemblies they serve. Then it would simply be a great shame to have received the gift of literacy and not to have exercised it fully. Creation-faith asserts that this world is made and held by God. For any Christian, one way to enact that faith is to delight in all that is or, at least, in as much of all that is as one can encounter in one lifetime. But for pastors, books and other tools of study remain marvelous ways to exercise and extend that encounter. The old idea of a *pastor's library* is still a worthy idea. Although such a library may now be supplemented with electronic materials, for the foreseeable future at least a few good books—books that can be held, marked, consulted, treasured, criticized, loaned to others—will remain indispensable.

This reading of books ought be no grim duty. *Delight* is the operative word. And the study that is called for is by no means only attention to useful subjects of immediate and pragmatic application to the next sermon, the next adult forum, or the next parish meeting. Pastors do really need to pay attention to *what is*—with curiosity following questions that genuinely interest them, apart from all utility, with joy delighting in the play of words and their interesting mediating relationships with other people's experiences of the world. Indeed, the postmodern approach to books will understand that they are always *authored*, always representing a point of view. Libraries are communities of people, expressing themselves, talking with each other across the ages, working within their own worldviews, sometimes lying, sometimes creating afresh, sometimes reflecting the truth as well as they can. The pastor, as a critical reader, will then know that words can hide as well as disclose and will know that engagement with these patterns of hiddenness and disclosure is part of what it is to encounter others and, with them, to encounter the world. Without such study, for the genuinely literate, life may be boring indeed. In fact, inability to find critical curiosity awakened may be one indication that a pastor is descending into depression and in need of rest and healing.

Delight does not mean constant happiness. *What is* includes stories of sorrow, the realities of broken systems and broken lives, the truth about human wretchedness and environmental degradation. Still, careful and honest attention to these matters as well can rightly draw the serious, even *enlivening* regard of the literate pastor.

The subjects that are possible for such study are endless. *Letter* and *Number* are two old Western ways of organizing kinds of knowledge. The *trivium* (the three studies of grammar, rhetoric, and dialectic, among which studies the ancients also placed poetry and philosophy) and the *quadrivium* (the four studies of arithmetic, geometry, music, and astronomy) organized these categories yet further. It may very well be that most pastors will tend toward being more at home on the *letter* or *trivium* side of this pattern, though we do need pastors who let their curiosity and skill at *number*—certainly at music, perhaps also at astronomy or, now, astrophysics—be increased. But more modern categories are also useful. The pastor may be reading in history, in psychology, in biography, in geography, in environmental studies, in comparative anthropology or ethnology, in aesthetics, architecture, or art history, in comparative literature, in sociology, in economics, in biology, in physics, in mechanical engineering, in chemistry, in political theory, in comparative religion, and on and on. Or, say it more directly. Without any useful need, a pastor may think, "What is this string-theory all about?" Or, "I want to know more about Japanese Noh theater." Or, "I have always wondered how my car's engine actually works." Or, "I want to know more about the history of baseball." Or, "What is really the largely suppressed story of the original peoples who lived in this very area where I am now living?"

Such interests belong, rightly, to the spirituality of a pastor when it is formed by the First Article of that baptismal symbol called the Creed.

And this is not yet to speak of novels and poetry and memoirs. Pastors may need to be reading novels or memoirs, especially if they are helped thereby to imagine the situation of other people and their interactions with the world. Indeed, brilliant fiction may often tell the most important truths in our times. In reading finely crafted fiction, a pastor may exercise the important skill of imagining the other. Then, the very other so imagined is potentially discovered by the reading pastor as another form of oneself, of the plural, layered identities we so strongly need to acknowledge: *we* are all the figures in the stories. Then poems, holding opposites together in beautiful or heart-breaking tension, may further help form our minds and lives so to hold together the often irreconcilable diversities they encounter. Other pastors may find these same gifts—imagining the other, delighting in words, holding one thing next to another—in other ways.

Such a range of possibilities for study should not be allowed to paralyze us. "How can I possible do this, given my schedule?" says the busy pastor. "Do you know how guilty I would feel?" Ah, dear sister or brother pastor, let the gospel of Christ deal with your guilt. Work hard, indeed. You need to do so. But then let that gospel call you to rest. Take time off, sabbath time. And let creation faith form you to pay attention to what is, taking new delight in your own encounter with parts of the world beyond your immediate organizing responsibility. Besides, you do not need to pick up the whole library of books. One book at a time—or maybe two—read even just a little every day—even just a page or two before you go to sleep—will lead you farther than you might imagine into the possibility of holding utterly new ideas together in your mind. And—the pastor may say to herself or himself—may I please let myself be open to thinking a new idea.

Of course, attending to God's world does not by any means only involve books. *Study*, in the sense formed by the Creed, may also involve simply walking around your neighborhood and knowing it physically. Or it may involve more: taking a course in art, dismantling and rebuilding a motorcycle, trying out bird watching, learning Spanish from a neighbor, learning how to cook, getting involved in a grocery co-op, getting involved in sports, tracing the actual ecology and the actual water sources of your local community, getting a telescope and using it, orienteering, mountaineering, knowing at least a few films and plays as primary places of current world interpretation, going to museums and art galleries, woodworking, becoming especially proficient in one or two hobbies, and on and on. These things exist in the world, and they matter. Perhaps learning one's own local world by foot—if walking or running is physically possible for you—and by attentive, slow observation, through the seasons, around the odd corners, may be the most important study of all. Perhaps visiting a local museum or play may be more important than reading another book. You need to decide what is restful for you and what matters most for your own lively engagement with what *is* in the world.

While some writers have been telling us—and it is a powerful telling in our conflicted times—about other times when great libraries and official theories of tolerance allowed for many diverse people to live together in creative cultural difference—seventh- to twelfth-century Muslim Andalusia in what is today southern Spain, for example—Christian pastors ought to be, in themselves and in the name of God, *now*, little islands of such cultural and intellectual generosity. Pastors ought to know about thinking, honoring, even *loving* two or more contrary ideas at the same time, refusing rigid intolerance while not losing their courage to express convictions. Such intellectual facility may indeed also assist in forming pastors toward personal practices of hospitality. In any case, such intellectual facility ought not be understood as cognitive weakness. On the contrary, the possibility of entertaining ideas in tension brings to one important expression the very spirituality of paradox that we have been exploring.

Still, anyone engaged in study should remember that there are media that lie and lie convincingly. There are bad books, ancient and modern. There are charlatans who teach. There are films or televised dramas that tell shallow stories with easy endings, simply as an occasion for the more engaging advertisements, the sales pitches, that are the real point of the show. It may be, for a pastor, that watching television can be one way of seeing what is actually in the world. But a pastor should be careful here. Mostly—though by no means entirely!—there is not much new on television that you cannot understand or figure out after only a brief exposure. Televison watching, like film going or Web surfing or any such overwhelming and bewitching media in which you may even temporarily give up your own control, should be engaged only critically. Generally, it really would be better—and the act of a profound spirituality—to turn off the television and engage in a conversation or go for a walk or read a book. Stepping out of that electronic world of sales will be like letting in the fresh air. But pastors need to be encouraged as well to be willing to stop reading a bad book or to get up and leave a bad movie. Literacy also involves the practice of lived criticism and the discriminate use of time. There are too many good books or good films—or good walks or possible conversations!—for us to waste the precious hours of another irreplaceable day.

But, again, be careful: "good" is a tricky word. Such discrimination should not be used to allow us to turn away from something that makes us uncomfortable, when we may need to broaden our worldview to include it. Nor should a pastor refuse to relax or hesitate to read a trash novel or a light mystery or never watch a sporting event or a B-film. These, too, are part of God's world. Entertainment is also good. The resolutions of a simple story, the play of a good and honest game, and the laughter of an uncomplex humor should not be scorned. It is simply that, in North American culture and in its widely exported patterns, we have been entertaining ourselves into numbness, inattention, oblivion, and death. We have let the shallow storylines and the world of sales be taken for granted as the climate of our days. In too many homes—perhaps, especially in parsonages and rectories—the television is on night and day. We need to take charge of our own attention again.

In regard to *attention*: it will be useful for pastors to consider whether talk in the church—in sermons, in parish education, or in informal conversation—about the plots of television programs or the fate of sporting teams (Super Bowl Sunday!) is exactly evidence of a gracious attention given to the actual circumstances of people's lives or whether a silence about these things may be a helpful invitation for people to pay attention to a larger world than entertainment, a helpful abstaining from further advertisements. The answer may be different in different places, but the question should be considered.

Sources of national and international news may need to be read or viewed with an especially critical eye. Television news has increasingly tended toward becoming itself an entertainment medium, competing to keep the market-share of viewers and thus to keep the advertisers. Local newspapers are frequently very limited in their coverage. And, a literate pastor should remember, all the news is also *authored*, carrying a particular point of view, sometimes editing or even lying to support that point of view. Still, reading a newspaper—or listening to fine, critical, multifaceted broadcast news or finding good electronic news sources, including those from other countries and other cultures—is immensely important for the pastor who is formed in creation faith.

But the Creed we confess does not stop at the First Article. Our baptism has also drawn us into a community that trusts the God who is saving the world. "We give you thanks for your Son," prays that church, "at the heart of human life, near to those who suffer, beside the sinner, among the poor, with us now." Again, the baptismal gift of this salvation faith may be lived out in a great diversity of ways in the lives of Christians. We have explored some of them, including the intercessions and the collection and especially the sending of the liturgy.

For pastors, however, such faith also entails study. The Second Article of the Creed draws a pastor into the ongoing, vital theological conversation of the times. "*What is this?*" was Luther's surprising, yet classic catechetical question to the creedal assertions. There have been others: "Why did God become a human being?" asks one, the root question of the *atonement* in Anselm's late eleventh-century reflections. "What does any of this mean for us?" might be the more likely inquiry of our day. All of these questions belong to the pastor.

Among the subjects of study in the spirituality of the pastor, the classic topics of theology will take a major place. A pastor may be reading, conversing, learning, studying in biblical criticism, dogmatics, pastoral theology, ecclesiology, liturgical theology, church history, and on and on. It will not be enough to rest on the few books one read quickly in seminary. Lively engagement with one current, important book in one or the other of these subjects may also help the pastor to be an engaged and interesting teacher in the parish. But again, while literacy in these matters may be important for a wise preacher, teacher, and counselor, the primary goal here is not utilitarian. The questions matter. They belong to a lively engagement with what is, seen from a Christian point of view. Indeed, they belong to the spirituality of religious questioning, of critical engagement with the symbols of faith, with which we began.

It may be especially crucial for a pastor to be reading the four Gospels of the New Testament again, thinking of their rich, diverse, and complex witness to Jesus, thinking of what the Gospels were and are actually intended to do. Similarly, it may be important for the pastor to be critically, freshly reading again the entire, fascinating, complex, and stunning corpus of the Bible: against the perceptions of fundamentalism, the Bible is itself a library of books quite capable of holding more than one idea together between one set of covers! Further, it probably will be especially essential for the pastor to be once again trying to answer Anselm's question—how might we today speak of the atonement, of the significance of Jesus' death?—and to be working on articulating the central significance of trinitarian theology. In the atonement inquiry, Anselm's own answer about Jesus being the substitute object of the Father's wrath will not be of much help to us, in spite of its becoming conventional in theological and hymnic language. Nor will Abelard's answer lead us very far: we do not so much need to be *like* Jesus as to receive his astonishing gift. Rather, much more help will be found in the ancient and now renewed reflections about God's coming among our suffering and death in Christ, so transforming them into places of life and hope. In the trinitarian inquiry, it will be important to refuse to regard the Trinity as an unspeakable puzzle in the sky, finding trinitarian theology to be instead words about God with us and God around us, as the story of Jesus' baptism so richly testifies. In addition, for the pastor the meaning of the liturgy—liturgical theology—and the meaning of the assembly that does liturgy—ecclesiology—will also be especially compelling subjects.

In any case, reading one or two books at a time, slowly, critically, setting aside the bad or shallow ones—or engaging in a study group or a class or a regular conversation—the pastor ought to be seeking again and again to articulate for himself or herself who God is, what Christianity is really about, why it matters, and how it responds to a world full of hope and sorrow, full of both fierce beauty and real evil.

And sometimes the pastor will rest, also intellectually. The truth of God and of salvation faith do not finally depend upon my ability to articulate them, though—paradoxically—I will continue to give my best efforts to doing so. But sometimes it will be important simply to rely upon a wider community—upon the words of old hymns, of another theologian, of a parishioner, of a chance conversation, of someone who announces the gospel to you—to speak for you, to hold you in faith.

In order to engage in such study, some pastors find that they want the discipline of a structured study program: to work for a degree or a certificate in an accredited school. The requirements of such a program can significantly help to balance the demands of daily parish responsibilities, making both the parish and the pastor more peaceful about the energy and the time needed for this intellectual work. More importantly, however, the company of other students and of accomplished teachers can be a remarkable gift. Also in study, pastors are not and ought not be alone. Even so, such a pastor-scholar will need to remember that, for her or for him, study belongs first of all to the spirituality of assembly office, to the implications of the faith of the Creed, and not to some imagined world of academic advancement. Furthermore, it will be important not to let the requirements of any program dull the significance of *delight*. Better to read one book with real curiosity and interest than to finish an insipid, perhaps even a *narrowing* program, especially if that program is primarily focused on today's popular but evanescent techniques rather than on classic questions, classic sources, and burning world needs.

Even were a degree program to be finished, the lifelong catechumenate goes on. The new Master or Doctor or certificate-bearer should savor and welcome the congratulations and good wishes of others: that rejoicing also belongs to the goodness of the world. But then the study goes on. Furthermore, according to the liturgical spirituality this book is seeking to explore, there is no higher—or lower!—title than *pastor* or *presider*. The pastor does not need to be "Dr. So-and-So," also not on the church stationary, let alone on the parish bulletin. And the colors and marks of academic achievement do not belong in the assembly, where the pastor wears a

THE PASTOR

simple baptismal garment—an alb—together with such other garments—a stole? a chasuble?—as signify liturgical office in the tradition of that assembly.

But program or no program, with books or in attention to experience, study belongs to the life of a pastor.

PRAYER THAT LIVES WITH THE CHURCH

So does prayer. Study does not exhaust the life of the pastor. The same Creed we have been exploring as forming creation and salvation faith—a faith that comes to expression in one small way in the study of the pastor—also forms us in the trust that God enlivens with the Spirit the community of the church. That faith, as well, comes to expression in manifold ways in the lives of Christians, not least in the need all Christians have to assemble together on the Lord's Day. Similarly, Third-Article faith, faith in the church-enlivening Spirit, is expressed in the need Christians have to work, serve, and think together with each other and to trust what is sometimes called the mutual comfort and consolation of the community. But, for the pastor, the Third Article of the Creed also entails prayer together with the church.

Every Christian is invited to pray. The Christian community has classically understood itself as a priesthood standing together before God, interceding for the needs of the world. Furthermore, the rhythm of Sunday assembly, marking the week with the resurrection gospel and with its thanksgivings and its intercessions, has flowed out into the life of the week with an answering rhythm of daily prayer, morning and evening, whereby at least some Christians mark the cardinal points of the day with signs of the gospel, with the praise of God, and with prayers for the life of the world. Even when a Christian participates very modestly in that rhythm—a few prayers at table, a Lord's Prayer at bedtime, an urgent prayer at a time of the neighbor's illness or a friend's death—she or he still stands before God as a member of the priesthood. She or he still claims and lives from that astonishing, over-the-top promise of the Jesus of the Gospels, "Ask, and it will be given you" (Matt. 7:7). Christian prayer may thus be a quite personal matter, but it is never alone, never individualist. Christians pray with Jesus Christ, in the power of the Spirit. They thus pray with those who are "in Christ," with those whom the Spirit enlivens and in whom the Spirit groans (Rom. 8:23). They pray with the church.

108

Pastors simply join the other Christians in this common—and remarkable—exercise of faith. There is nothing particularly different about the pastor's prayer. Only, since the pastor often presides in the Sunday prayer of the assembly, she or he will be especially aware of the way that prayer through the week flows out of the Sunday meeting, marks Sunday meaning on each day, continues the church's voice of praise, and builds again and again the list of real needs for which we will pray again next week. Pastors will also feel a continued need to pray for the people of the assemblies they serve and to pray for all those other people they meet in the course of being pastors. People do often look to pastors as holy figures. One of the ways pastors know this symbolic interaction as broken to the purpose of the gospel is this: they give those people to God in prayer, not being God or not being even particularly holy enough to be much help themselves. Furthermore, pastors need the classic rhythms of the day and week and year, the rhythms that come to expression not only in the weekly assembly but also in the church's daily prayer, in order to read the Scripture well and prepare well for the next meeting of the church.

So the pastor prays with the church. In the exercise of prayer, she or he may indeed serve as a model for other Christians, though that is not the reason for so praying. The pastor needs to do this herself or himself. Indeed, the very idea that it is *prayer with the church* helps here. It is not the unique prayer-life of the pastor that matters. Rather, pastors are beggars who join with other beggars, trusting the task and the promises that have been given to the community. Pastors join a prayer that exists already before they pray.

Such prayer that lives with the church may be joined in many ways. The classic way is to make use of the daily office, a structure of prayer that marks especially the morning and evening of each day with psalmody, a hymn, a Scripture reading, a Gospel canticle (Magnificat at evening and Benedictus at morning) and intercessions. Evening prayer may precede this structure with a *lucernarium*, a ritual lighting of lamps focused on Christ as Light, and morning prayer may conclude it with a proclamation of the resurrection and a thanksgiving for baptism. The use of this office is canonically incumbent upon the clergy in some communions. It ought to be received as a gift and a possibility by those in other churches. In any case, the current worship books of the Lutheran, Presbyterian, Episcopal, and Roman Catholic churches can be used to fill out and easily keep this structure. So, for any user of this daily office, this liturgy of the hours, the psalms, with their pungent combination of poetic praise and particular lament, can form an ongoing school of honest and beautiful prayer. The best of the hymns can then echo the psalms, marking night and morning with articulate Christian faith. The ecumenical daily lectionary of the Consultation on Common Texts can guide the readings, echoing the Sunday readings of the Revised Common Lectionary and so linking daily prayer with the intention of the Sunday assembly. Mary's Song—or that of Zechariah—can celebrate that the Incarnate One who grounds those songs—the One who fills the hungry with good things or gives the rising dawn—also now is at the heart of these readings. Then the newspaper and parish life—in any case, real needs throughout the world—can guide the prayers. This whole complex makes up a remarkable and lively structure.

But, with a knowledge of this structure, one can also keep this office by using only a Bible and a hymnal. Or, much more modestly and in a modesty appropriate to some of our days, one can also pray in the pattern of the daily office simply by thanking God for the darkness and the light in the darkness at night, praising God for the resurrection at dawn, and then at either time praying as well as one can for the needy world. As Anne Lamott says, "Thank you, Thank you, Thank you" and "Help me, Help me, Help me" are also profound prayers, or, in our terms, prayers within the deepest language of the praying community, prayers with the church.

But a wise pastor will at least sometimes seek to do this prayer not so much alone as with others. Parishes may indeed consider making daily morning or evening prayer part of what is available in congregational life. More simply, midweek evening prayer may mark certain seasons of the year. In any case, the structure of the office and the pattern of its use through the year belong to all Christians. It is done in their name, whether or not very many people engage in it.

The pastor's prayer with the church may take other forms as well: the Moravian Daily Texts, for example, together with their accompanying hymn-texts, or bedtime prayers in the family, or hymns and more hymns, new and old, sung alone or with one's family and often learned by heart, or the regular exercise of the so-called Jesus Prayer, especially if it is prayed interiorly on the street or in public places, in the name of those one meets or passes, or bedside prayers with the sick, or acts of thanksgiving and beseeching that flow through every event of the day, or meditative reading of Scripture that leads to prayer, or simply the Psalter itself, perhaps prayed through slowly, psalm by psalm, day by day, starting round again at Psalm 1 after Psalm 150 is reached. And prayer at table: even if no other prayer is possible, the pastor's table will be marked by straightforward acts of thanksgiving for food and beseeching for the hungry of the world: "Come Lord Jesus, be our guest and let these gifts to us be blessed. Blessed be God who is our Bread. May all the world be clothed and fed," runs one such prayer.

It is not that the pastor's prayers are unique or exemplary. It is also not a matter of how much the pastor prays. It is rather that she or he prays with the church. Each of these forms of prayer will be the more profound if they are not approached as new or heroic efforts, as a ladder up to God, but as gifts that already exist, as a communal practice shared with many other people, as a place of grace and truth into which the pastor may also enter. Formed by the Creed in the trust that the Spirit does indeed enliven a community as it uses the holy things of the gospel and called to preside in the midst of one assembly of that community, the pastor finds the prayers of that community spilling out into the week, interacting with daily life and the real world and gathering up the pastor's own spirit in their flow. That flow is honest-to-God about both the beauty and the utter need of the world. And that flow—the Creed teaches us to trust—is the very flow of the Spirit of God, praying with our spirit, gathering us into the work of the church on behalf of all the world.

When I was a young man, I thought seriously about becoming a monk. I was partly drawn to the monastic life because of its utter seriousness about communal prayer. I suppose that I was also partly drawn for aesthetic reasons: the remarkably beautiful, old church building of the community I was considering, the poetry of the nights and days interpreted in common song, and the anchored reality of these particular people living for the rest of their lives on this particular, beautiful land.

For a variety of reasons, I did not become a monk, in that community or in any other. Perhaps I was not up to it. Perhaps there was a wider, for me truer, beauty that drew me. I do not know. Still, I have continued to admire many communities of monks and I have continued to find ways that monastic spirituality has often preserved treasures of liturgical life that could help us all. But I did ultimately—and after a long journey—become a pastor. I made another sort of promise, amid another community. In the process, I discovered two things about those monastic gifts I have so much admired. One was that the communal prayer I had found so beautiful—the daily office—belonged to the whole church and not just to the monks. In fact, it had belonged to local congregations and to people who regularly gathered to pray in their name long before it had come to mark communities of ascetics. It is a gift to us all. We can use it. It can hold a pastor in the prayer of the church.

The other discovery was this: the anchored beauty of living the rest of your life in a real place also belongs to us all. It belongs to authentic Christian life in this world. The stable, real place, in all its acute beauty and terror, in all its particular reality, is this earth.

A remnant from the time of my struggle with a monastic vocation has been my fascination with the lucid, elegant little monastic rule written by frère Roger of Taizé. In fact, phrases from that rule have often intertwined with my life, giving me words by which to live, words with which to hope. One of my favorite such passages is this:

> Open yourself to all that is human and you will find that every vain desire to escape from the world disappears. Be present to your age; adapt yourself to the conditions of the moment. Father, I pray you not to take them out of the world, but to keep them from evil.

It is wonderfully paradoxical, with a paradox that belongs to the Christian spirituality of the questions, that a text from a monastic rule should invite both monks and those who are moved by their lives to forget about escaping from the world. Indeed, frère Roger's little text speaks with an authentic Christian voice. Echoing the playwright Terrence, didn't old Tertullian argue that nothing that is human is alien to the Christian. In any case, Bishop Grundtvig of Denmark asserted that he was a human being first and a Christian second.

I am much moved by these witnesses and their stability in this good, needy earth. I have wanted to be a pastor—not a monk, but a pastor—in the hope of this text. I have wanted my prayer to be here, in praise and petition, with the real community of the church, amid the reality of this earth, before the God who loves the world. And I have longed for my study to explore and delight and mourn and rejoice in the same actual and embraced stability—in all that is, in God's good world.

6

The Pastor in Daily Living

The Commandments

What else is to be said about the life of a pastor? Amid all the differences and particularities of the various pastors' lives, what more might be said in common about their shared spirituality? They study. They pray. What else?

Like many other Christians, they live from the liturgy. That is, they find in the gospel of Jesus Christ, celebrated in community, a new orientation toward daily life—new courage to live in hope and forgiveness, new devotion toward the needs of others and toward justice and peace, new commitment toward the care and stewardship of the good things of the earth. These perspectives are not so much ideals to be achieved as genuine possibilities that emerge in ordinary life because of its reinterpretation by the central matters of Christian liturgy. The surprising words read and sung in the assembly give to the participants, including the pastor, a story by which to live. The prayers of the church invite us all—the pastor included—to find our days marked by both thanksgiving and beseeching. The communal remembrance of baptism gives a recovered identity with which to walk in the world—a communal identity, but paradoxically one that does not shut other people out. Because of the cross, baptism gives the baptized an identification with the wretched of the world. Because of the resurrection, baptism gives a way to live without self-protecting fear, a way available also to the pastor. And the shared meal of Jesus gives a continually renewed way to approach all daily food and all daily community—"bread and forgiveness," these are called in the Lord's Prayer—with thanksgiving and mutual care. The pastor, who is frequently responsible for the central communal exercise of these symbols, also receives them as gifts: it is a good thing, for example, for the pastor to be given the Holy Communion by another. The pastor also lives from these gifts, as does any believer.

Each of these gifts from the symbolic practices of the Christian assembly has something of redirection or reorientation about it. In the stories of the Bible, in Baptism and in the Supper, in the announcement of the forgiveness of sins and in the proclamation of the resurrection, Christians believe that God has dealt with us in new, world-changing ways, ways that change our understanding of who God is as well as our ideas of how to live before this God. It is as if each of us—and the whole assembly together—play the role of Raguel, the father of the bride in the great deuterocanonical story of Tobit. In that story, after the newlyweds are found alive and not dead—and it was certainly death that was expected—Raguel gives thanks to God in these words: "Blessed are you because you have made me glad. It has not turned out as I expected, but you have dealt with us according to your great mercy" (Tob. 8:16). The life that flows from such grateful surprise will itself be redirected toward forgiveness, hope, generosity to others, and at least some gestures of countercultural resistance. God's constantly surprising mercy reorients us all toward the practice of mercy in our lives. Of course, it is a major responsibility of the pastor to see to it that the world-changing mercy of God comes to expression in the liturgy of the assembly. But now we can reflect on how the pastor also is invited to live out of that same surprise.

A Symbol for the Reoriented Life

So consider the meaning of the Ten Commandments. In the classic catechism, those centrally symbolic texts that represented the baptismal process, the Commandments, have stood for the call to a changed life that Christians think belongs, in one way or another, to the baptismal vocation. The ancient catechumenate seems to have begun with an inquiry about whether the candidate for baptism was willing to live a new kind of life, a life reoriented away from ancient social standards and toward a reflection and celebration of the mercy of God. Would the candidate be willing to visit orphans and widows, for example, instead of giving public offerings in the temples of the gods, or be willing to care for the sick and imprisoned, instead of going to see the pomp and killing of the gladiatorial games? The Commandments, with their challenges to both idolatry and murder, were important teaching texts in this inquiry. Modern teaching of the faith has asked similar questions when it has sought to explore the outlines of a Christian ethics and sought to ask whether being baptized makes any difference at all in our current world. Now as in the past, it is as if Jesus has stood before anyone who has wished to be baptized—or anyone who has wished to relearn and live out of baptism—as he stood before the inquiring man of Mark 10. To the question, "What must I do to inherit eternal life?" Jesus responds, "You know the commandments..." (Mark 10:17-19). So countless Christians have rehearsed these old legal prohibitions and requirements, asking what they might mean for their own lives.

But there are problems with using this text from the past. Are not these commandments simply one small part of an ancient, outdated Near Eastern patriarchal code, preserved in the Old Testament and addressed only to free, land-owning males? Can they really be made to say anything useful to present life? Even more, far from being symbols of baptism, have they not now become symbols of the current culture wars in the United States? By being placed on courthouse walls and statehouse lawns, have they not come to stand for a certain kind of bourgeois reading of the values needed to sustain the social status quo, keeping power in the hands of those who already have power? Have they not been politicized? Furthermore, even if they could be made to speak a trenchant word to the present time, would they not simply accuse us? This law—especially as, say, the Matthean Jesus teaches it, astronomically heightening its requirements—leaves none of us able to consider ourselves righteous, all of us being idolaters and murderers, adulterers and liars, by the reckoning of the Sermon on the Mount. Even the Markan Jesus responds with both love and an overwhelming requirement—that all possessions be sold and the proceeds given away to the poor (Mark 10:21)—to the man who thought he had kept all the commandments. In Mark's story, the result of that heightened requirement is sadness and failure. Then what does this law have to do with actually shaping our lives? And, finally, what does it have to do especially with the shaping of pastors' lives?

These questions should not be waved away. They belong to a serious re-reading of the Commandments themselves. Indeed, they belong to the paradoxes and questions of a healthy Christian spirituality. A faithful Christian reading of the Ten Commandments in our time requires these questions.

But the fascinating thing is that these "ten words" have functioned together as a symbol since quite ancient times and, as a *symbolic* text, they have been subject to continuous reinterpretation. The Jesus of the Gospels himself already seems to be engaged in such reinterpretation. Indeed, long before the Gospels the very insertion of these communal laws within the biblical story of the exodus reinterpreted moral and legal requirements as flowing from God's act of merciful liberation: "I am the LORD your God, who brought you out of the land of Egypt, out of the house of slavery," the commandments are made to begin (Exod. 20:2). Communal order is seen to follow and reflect the ways that God has acted to save and recreate the world itself. The Hebrew prophets continued this reinterpretation by inviting the community to behold the "neighbor" of the text of the Commandments, especially the poor neighbor, in new ways.

Then, in the baptismal practice of the church, the Commandments have symbolized the general call to a life that is reoriented in the world according to God's life-giving, world-making mercy in Christ. They have been able to stand for the life that follows in gratitude for the gifts of mercy received in Word and Sacrament. In the early centuries, the Commandments were, in certain ways, taken literally—in the refusal of public idolatry and murder, for example—and in other ways not—as in the dropping of the sabbath commandment or the reinterpretation, through much struggle, of the prohibition of images. Because of the incarnation, Christians came to argue, the churches *do* make images of God, though always with the critique of images hovering near.

One of the most creative of the interpreters of these "words" was Martin Luther. In his explanations of the Commandments, set out in his Small Catechism, the Commandments do far more than forbid certain actions. Rather, rewritten in terms that were refreshing and new in sixteenth-century Germany, they invite the reader to an interesting, graceful life-before-God in this present, real world. The false-witness commandment, for example, is understood not only to forbid public lying about our neighbors but to encourage us to "speak well of them, and interpret everything they do in the best possible light." The commandment against coveting is seen to invite us away from falsely founded lawsuits—or perhaps from lawsuits at all. And, while the sabbath commandment is clearly maintained, its explanation does not even mention the sabbath as the day of rest. Rather, it invites us to that assembly where there is reading and preaching of God's Word. One could argue that Luther calls for attention to hearing the Word of God out of the deep, biblically formed idea that only that Word, heard in trusting faith, will actually bring us to true rest (see Heb. 4:1-11; Ps. 95:7-11), something anxious law observance will never do. In any case, these are creative reinterpretations, arising from the sense that baptismal vocation is vocation to a reoriented life.

The Ten Commandments are a symbol of this reoriented life. And the work of their interpretation must go on, into our present day, inquiring about the significance of these summary words in our own time, criticizing their misuse, and doing both in company with interpreters throughout the ages. In their biblical and baptismal uses, the "ten words" can and have been read as surprising and countercultural in intent. They ought, by no means, be surrendered to become simply an icon of political or social conservatism or a lawn ornament of self-righteousness. Conservatism is a legitimate political choice, but for a Christian it must go paired with self-criticism and not with an assertion of divine sanction, founded in a literalist reading of Scripture. Indeed, the earliest biblical use of the Commandments was as a celebration of the God who liberated slaves from their supposed owners, hardly a conservative act. This insertion of moral requirements into the deliverance story requires us to think about them, engage with them, reinterpret them for present life.

Of course, a responsibly reinterpreted Commandment will then the more stringently accuse us. We fail. We will continue to fail, egregiously. But the demands of the law are nonetheless important. We must fall again on the mercy of God, knowing ourselves no better than anyone else—no better than the worst sinners—in our ethical efforts. But, paradoxically, that very mercy restores us, invites us again to see the world anew, invites us again to live. The Ten Commandments can stand for the accusation of our sin. They can also stand as a symbol for the new life that is God's continual gift. In such a way they are indeed a baptismal symbol, showing forth our death and illuminating something of life-as-a-gift. It is not so much that they tell us the precise steps we should follow as that they invite us again into living the reorientation we were given when we were joined with Jesus Christ in baptism, when we were delivered by the exodus that is in him.

What follows here is a brief consideration of some of the characteristics of that baptismal death and of that baptismal reorientation in the world. These reflections are set out as part of a pastor's spirituality partly because a pastor bears significant teaching authority in the church, a teaching authority that needs to be exercised in, among other things, the ongoing reinterpretation of the Commandments. But they are set out as part of a pastor's spirituality also because there are at least a few specific ways that both the gift and the requirement of the law may address a pastor and a pastor's life.

The Pastor before God

In the medieval way of numbering the Commandments, the first three deal with the community's relationship with God: "You shall have no other gods," "You shall not make wrongful use of the name of the LORD your God," and "Remember the sabbath day, and keep it holy." Of course, this numbering already represents an interpretation, the image-making prohibition (Exod. 20:4-5a) being subsumed under the First Commandment. Roman Catholic and Lutheran catechisms follow this numbering, while the later catechisms of an an-iconic Reformed Christianity frequently do not, including rather *four* commandments in this first table of the law. In any case, the Christian discussion of this set of words has included an ongoing struggle about the nature of idolatry as well as a concern about the appropriate use of both religious language and festivals.

What shall we say of these words? What do they propose to the pastor's life? How shall pastors think of them for themselves and not only for those they teach?

The refusal of idolatry should be clear enough. Christians join with both Jews and Muslims in declaring that there is only one God. Still, what might it be to "have a god," as the Commandment calls the matter? Some recent commentators have invited us to consider all the things that are of ultimate concern in our lives. Are they our gods? No matter how good a thing may be, from the point of view of the Commandment it needs to be relativized before the only Holy One. Perhaps work or success or self-realization or children or family or ethnic identity or doctrinal purity or social activism or political conviction or even the congregation itself have become as gods for us. These idolatries are quite possible for pastors. And, to the extent that pastors often possess temptations toward addictive practices—with alcohol or sex or work, to name a few—perhaps the objects of these addictions are our gods, way more important to us than the appearance of any divine image in any Hindu temple is to its worshipers.

The First Commandment accuses us.

So do the other two. It may not be so much that pastors curse and swear. But religious lying, phony preaching, pretense at authority in God's name when there is none—these are pastoral practices. And many, many pastors fail to come to regular, deep and lively rest, letting all else go, thereby celebrating and trusting that God made the world (Exod. 20:11) and redeemed it (Deut. 5:15). Indeed, it is a tricky matter for pastors that the very assembly around the Word that Luther proposed as the proper Christian response to the sabbath commandment is, for pastors, a workplace. For a wearied and discouraged pastor it may be hard to say of that Word-in-assembly, as Luther said, that they keep it holy "and gladly hear and learn it."

But the accusations may be deeper still. Precisely when a pastor may be able to say that he or she loves church, preaches and listens both gladly and carefully, lives with a deep sense of God's presence, has no addictions, takes breaks, and tries to keep all other priorities in relative order before God, these words will still accuse. All of these things are good. But God is God, not our idea of God, not our self-in-order before God, not our own ideas of pure religion or of real rest.

So, dear pastor, creep back to the water. These accusations are true, and they do cast the shadow of your own failure, sin, and death. But, united with Christ, your death is already there in that water, and you have been forgiven and raised to new life. Hear that word spoken to you—by your neighbor, your friend, your spouse, this book, the next liturgy in which you participate. The Spirit of the Risen One blows in that Word and from that water as well, and that Spirit keeps forming you for living—not dying—together with us all.

We cannot say here what the Spirit will be doing. This book is not intended as a law book. But, reflecting on these same Commandments, we can make some guesses about the kind of interesting life that may be opened before you. Perhaps the continuing end of idolatry may best be signified by a lively sense of humor. Perhaps you will find yourself both taking your responsibilities with great seriousness and, at the same time, welcoming the moments when some trickster or some unintended mistake messes up your excellent constructions. Perhaps you will see that the Second Commandment invites you to the critique of all religion, all use of the divine names, including especially your own. Perhaps you will find that keeping festivals with others—the Sunday assembly, but also the Three Days of the paschal feast, and Christmas, the Christian version of winter solstice singing, and then all of the liturgical year, as also the other festivals of your own culture or your own family—will be newly life giving, rest making for you. Indeed, perhaps you will refuse to participate in or to enable the annual pre-Christmas madness and instead take and teach new delight in Advent. In any case, you will be discovering, in the gift of the Spirit, that the reoriented life flowing from baptism and from the assembly's gifts—the life these Commandments may symbolize—will have something of the countercultural about it. It will resist making central anything our present culture idolizes. It will criticize religious self-importance or self-assurance. It will delight in rest and festivity and not only endless production. And you will be discovering that "being-before-God"—the very matter these commandments are seeking to delineate—has been given to you already as a gift: this same Spirit draws you into life with Jesus Christ, the One who shares all death and loss, and into life with Jesus Christ's own people, and so draws you before the very face of God. And God says of you: "My child, my beloved." These gifts for daily living are present for the pastor.

THE PASTOR WITH OTHERS

The remaining seven Commandments, the second table, deal with the community's relationships with each other: "Honor your father and your mother," "You shall not murder," "You shall not commit adultery," "You shall not steal," "You shall not bear false witness against your neighbor," "You shall not covet your neighbor's house," and "You shall not covet . . . anything that belongs to your neighbor."

Of course, this way of listing the Commandments already involves a reinterpretation of the text. We have here left out the idea that the neighbor's wife—not to mention the neighbor's slaves—is to be considered property (Exod. 20:17), protected property indeed, but still property, right alongside the neighbor's animals. But it is right to make this omission, Christians having come to believe that people are not rightly considered as objects to be owned. Indeed, the baptismal assertion of Paul—"There is no longer Jew or Greek, there is no longer slave or free, there is no longer male and female; for all of you are one in Christ Jesus" (Gal. 3:28)—shakes the foundations of such ownership and of patriarchy generally. Furthermore, the promise of long life in the promised land if one honors one's parents (Exod. 20:12) is omitted, both because Christians are uneasy with the "if you are good, then you will be rewarded" schema as far too unrealistic about human suffering, but also because "the land," for Christians, has got to include every place on the earth.

But, given these initial interpretations and given the ongoing history of interpretation, what shall we say now of these words? What do they propose to the pastor's life? How shall pastors think of them for themselves as well as for those they teach?

Again, the forbidding of murder, adultery, theft, lying about somebody else, and coveting somebody else's stuff is clear enough. So is the counsel to honor one's parents. Among pastors there are certainly some public sinners who have openly engaged in all of these forbidden things and are profoundly in need of being restrained and, if it is possible, being forgiven and being reformed. But, in the reflections of the prophets and then again in the preaching of the Matthean Jesus and the interpretations of Martin Luther, these requirements have been greatly heightened. Pastors need to think about the ways in which they, *as pastors*, keep silent in the face of a murderous war, engage in a little quiet lust after sexually desirable people who are in their care, take more reimbursement of expenses or more tax breaks than they are in fact owed, participate in gossip and character assassination, saying things that they do not know to be true and saying them without checking with the person in question, and covet a better call with better benefits—perhaps a new car or a new computer or a second house. And pastors, in being pastors, do not always honor their parents: how does one put together the Commandment and the sayings of Jesus about hating one's father and mother? Keeping the Commandments is not a simple thing.

These words accuse us.

And they may do so more deeply still. Say the pastor's conscience is clear. Say this pastor has had a wonderful and rare relationship with his or her parents: they are proud and supportive and have all they want of respect and support from their child. Say this pastor speaks out on social-justice matters, observes personal sexual boundaries, is scrupulous with finances, always goes to the others before talking about them—as Matthew 18 advises—and takes a certain joy in practicing simplicity. All of these things are good—wonderful even. But the words still accuse. The neighbor—the profound mystery of the other—remains there, beyond the ability of the best-ordered life, as profoundly *other* as is God. There are countless people who have died in agony today, have been raped today, maligned today, violently robbed today, and I have not been able to help. Perhaps

I have not even wanted to help. How is it that my conscience is so clear? Am I blind? Is my world so circumscribed that I do not see our communal guilt? No matter how simple my life, I participate in a system that robs and kills. "We abuse, we betray, we are cruel. We destroy, we embitter, we falsify. We gossip, we hate, we insult…," says one of the classic confessions of the Day of Atonement, rightly continuing to fill out the whole alphabet with our continual communal wrongs.

But do not let this accusation turn you to cynicism or immobility. Say it again: dear pastor, creep back to the water. These accusations are true, and they do cast the shadow of your own failure, sin, and death. But, united with Christ, your death is already there in that water and you have been forgiven and raised to new life. Hear that word spoken to you—by your neighbor, your friend, your spouse, this book, the next liturgy in which you participate. The Spirit of the Risen One blows in that Word and from that water as well, and that Spirit keeps forming you for living—not dying—together with us all.

Then, let us imagine something of what the Spirit might be doing with you as you live from this forgiveness and the end of fear. Perhaps—beside struggling with how to best honor your parents and, at the same time, be yourself and follow your calling—you will be honoring the ancestors much more widely, becoming, as George Herbert says, "a Lover of old Customs," delighting in the mothers and fathers you find that you have from many families, many different places, and many different cultures. They are there in your parish and in your neighborhood. Perhaps you will also discover what it is to honor your *children* and the children of others—not sentimentally nor permissively, but with real and deep respect, teaching and leading when they need it, letting go when it is time. Perhaps you will be using your leadership position to discuss with others much more seriously what a politically embraced theory of just war would mean for national and international life. Perhaps you will indeed delight in the attractive people around you—attractive in all sorts of ways—but you will laugh as you know that just as you admire a beautiful mountain or a beautiful seascape, you do not have to *have* it. Indeed, you cannot. Blessed be God for the goodness and beauty of life-in-the-flesh. Blessed be God for sex. And that is enough. No, more: perhaps you will be discovering how mutual forgiveness can restore your deepest relationships, how fidelity is life giving and life anchoring, how the closest ones to you are the best revelations of the astonishing mystery of the other. Perhaps you will start trying to stop stealing from the creation itself and from its fragile balances, doing so in whatever ways you can. Perhaps you will find new joy in apologizing for others. Perhaps you will be discovering and embracing something of the simple life, in your own way or in ways you discuss together in the church. And on and on. These are good possibilities for pastors, living real daily lives among others, on the earth, in the flesh, alive, unafraid.

In any case, formed by the Spirit who is given in Jesus' death and resurrection and poured out in your baptism, you will be discovering that life with the wonderful and mysterious and needy others—the very matter that these commandments seek to delineate—has been given to you already. Of course you are accused before them all. You are a sinner. Even a public sinner. But you are also forgiven. You are given a new, Spirit-led imagination for turning to the other. And you are thereby given not just the duty of attention to the others, but also their attention to you. You have been given participation in all of their virtues as well as in their needs. You cannot do it all. But you can live, fully, really, undeceived and unafraid. And when you are afraid, you can listen again to the word of mercy and the love of those around you. Christ comes to you, surrounds you, with all those who belong to him. And, though there are many, many others, all in need beyond your failing ability, out of sight is *not* out of mind. Christ minds.

When I was struggling with the question of becoming a monk, I came across a little text that was, at that moment and since, of profound help to me. It was written on a poster, put up in a Swiss airport, appealing for people who might want to study to become pilots. It was a quotation from the French author and aviator, Antoine de Saint-Exupéry, the man most famous for his book The Little Prince. *The quotation was not from that book. In fact, I do not know its actual source since I have never yet come across it in his writing. It did not in the slightest tempt me to become a pilot. But it did nonetheless help me. In French, it read: "Comme une soif profonde: le desir d'être un homme parmi les hommes." My rather literal translation would run, "As a profound thirst: the desire to be a human being among human beings."*

On first reading, the text seems rather obvious and unimportant, the kind of Gallic abstraction Americans can find annoying. Perhaps it struck me so much at the time because I was struggling with whether, for me, the religious vocation I was considering would involve abandoning life among other human beings, on ordinary human terms. I know, of course—I know now especially because of dear friends I have made since then—that religious vocations, including the vocations of many monks, do not at all necessarily involve abandoning your own humanity. But for me, at the time, the text seemed written in fire. And, in any case, I have also learned since then that being a human being among other human beings is not so obvious at all. Many, many people live as if they are alone, unsurrounded, as if located in very narrow horizons, concerned only for the self. I am sometimes among them.

But I also know that the profound thirst is slaked in the mercy of the triune God. In the life of the gospel, we are given many others. The goal for Christians ought not be to become divine, but, in that very holy mercy, to become fully human, alive in the network of humankind, living gladly on the earth, perhaps like the relationships of the triune God who always goes out toward the other, for the other. So, as we have seen, somewhere Augustine says of himself, "Insofar as I am a bishop, I am in danger; insofar as I am a believer, I am safe." More vividly yet, John Chrysostom said something like, "The road to hell is paved with priests' skulls." Ah, being a pastor or a priest is indeed dangerous, with all of its own unique and deadly ways of breaking the Commandments. But the pastor arises from and falls back into the company of believers, the assembly, the baptized, human beings who find themselves being pulled up from hell and made again fully human only by the grace of God, the company given ever-new possibility of genuinely interesting and engaged life.

I wish for you, dear pastor, joy in your office, but also serious awareness of its dangers. I also wish for you many moments of safety, and a growing glad awareness that you are a human being among human beings.

7

The Pastor in Dying

Baptism, the Supper, the Keys

One thing remains in a discussion of the spirituality of the pastor: death. The pastor also comes to die.

In this death and dying, of course, the pastor is exactly like everybody else. Pastors who contract deadly pneumonia or metastasized cancer suffer and die no differently than other people. Fatal accidents befall pastors as they do other people. Besides, everyone must also deal with the outriders of death, the harbingers of death or the little deaths we all suffer through the course of our lives. In many ways, these too are the same for pastors as for other folks. The ordained clergy also grow sick, bury their parents and then their friends, fail at some things they do, lose their spouses, leave or lose their jobs, move on to new places, find themselves aging, see their children go away, find their lives changing.

But, in another sense, pastors do have a particular kind of experience in the facing of death, unique to their vocation. They bear frequent responsibility in the community for presiding at funerals, at the communal remembrance and committal of the dead. People turn to them when facing their own deaths or the deaths of their beloved ones. More: pastors must teach clearly about the Christian approach to death. They must speak of death over and over again in preaching and in baptisms. They visit the sick, including the grievously sick. They include remembrance of the dead in the prayers and festivals of the church. It follows that such a presence of death in the regular practice of pastors, week in and week out, inevitably heightens their awareness of their own mortality. That presence may also tempt them to grow interiorly callous or professionally shallow toward death and dying, as a strategy of self-protection. Furthermore, those little deaths—those messengers of our own dying—come in some specific forms for pastors. Pastors must face such matters as leaving one call when accepting another, letting go of people they have helped, or accepting the limits of their ability to help at all.

Such matters also occupy the spirituality of the pastor, that way of living amid the symbols—with embraced paradoxes and profound religious questioning— that we have explored here. What shall we say then, in the face of this experience of death? We should simply be silent first, waiting, listening, honoring the sorrow, holding ourselves before the truth. But then we might also speak carefully and briefly, trying these proposals for a pastor's life: The liturgy itself involves a certain practice in dying. The little deaths of a pastor's life reinforce that practice. And the life-giving gospel of Jesus Christ—as it lives, not least of all, in the gracious symbols of Baptism, the Holy Supper, and the words of forgiveness—is also for the pastor herself or himself.

Practice in Dying

Paradoxically, living from the liturgy involves learning something about dying. Indeed, it can be said that faithful Christian liturgy inevitably involves its participants in something like practice or rehearsal for dying. Of course, the liturgy is overwhelmingly about living now, in forgiveness and hope, surrounded by the mercy of God. But that *living now*, in Christian conception, includes a steady honesty about death. And of course, the hard and messy work of actually dying is usually not evoked in Christian liturgy, the slow sense of suffocation and increasing pain and disconnection that makes up the reality of many, many deaths. But the fact of human death is constantly present, like the cross of Christ is constantly present, even if it cannot be fully encountered or described or understood, even if none of us is quite able to accept that we will really die. In cultures so given to hiding death, as are many cultures of our current world, the liturgy's straightforwardness is remarkable. In many ways, pastors are responsible for that straightforwardness, or at least they share responsibility for not obscuring the clarity of the liturgy's references to death and dying. And a pastor can draw on that clarity also to understand his or her own situation.

What clarity? In the lectionary for the Sunday liturgy it would be hard to find a single set of readings that does not have at least one mention of or allusion to death. The hymns of the church, on the whole, also possess a remarkable range of serious language for death. "Time, like an ever-rolling stream, soon bears us all away...," we sing, in Isaac Watts's widely used *O God Our Help in Ages Past*. "God is God, though all by death were taken...," sings out an old Norwegian hymn, perhaps most known in North America because of its central role in the film *Babette's Feast*, a film that can be taken to be largely about death and the little deaths of failure. Furthermore, the very reason for the Sunday meeting has to do with the death and resurrection of Jesus, articulated at every point in the service and placed before the assembly in clarity in the creeds. Taught by the language of the Scripture and the creeds, the preacher will also speak of death, avoiding the euphemisms so common in current speech. It would be painfully ludicrous to say that Jesus Christ "passed away." It is similarly inaccurate and unhelpful to so speak of the death of any of us.

But the clarity of the liturgy is deeper yet. At the heart of the Sunday assembly we are invited to receive the very signs of Jesus' death—the body and blood of Christ—but now as food for life. After we have done so, some liturgies invite us to sing like old Simeon in the *Nunc Dimittis* of Luke 2, asking that he now be allowed to die: "Now, Lord, you let your servant go in peace, your word has been fulfilled..." Here is a direct rehearsal of our death. More: as we recall that we are baptized, we know that we have already been drawn into death with Jesus Christ and are already being daily raised with him to new life in the Spirit. According to the old Eastern icon of the resurrection, the risen Christ is pulling Adam and Eve out of hell, and with them all humanity, clinging to their heels. Our baptism and our daily encounter with the word of God's promise are always filled with this same hell-emptying Christ. Now. The daily prayers of the church also draw us into the same reality: night prayer sometimes has us singing *Nunc Dimittis* at the end of the day, imagining our approaching sleep as a little death; morning prayer often has us singing as raised together with Christ who is the rising dawn of God's beloved world.

The classic liturgy of Christians gives us words and forms for honestly practicing death.

The intention of such liturgical practice should include neither morbidity nor fear. Christian faith trusts that God has overcome death, turning death into a place of life through Christ and giving us the Spirit of hope. Christian faith trusts that beyond each death is God and that God is trustworthy. Such faith invites us both to honesty about the fact that we die and, at the same time, a continual abandoning of fear. But note: such hope has nothing whatever to do with widespread popular conceptions of the immortality of the human spirit, as if the essence of the human being inevitably continues to exist even without any God, nor with media descriptions of the afterlife, as if we knew anything about it at all. No. The Christian confidence in the face of death, the confidence repeatedly rehearsed in the liturgy, is entirely based on confidence in the triune God, on the narrative of the death and resurrection of Jesus Christ as pulling us and our stories into the mercy of God. The Bible has very little in its pages about any *heaven*. The biblical "kingdom of heaven" is usually a circumlocution for that "kingdom of God" which is appearing now in the ministry of Jesus and in the outpouring of the Spirit from his death and resurrection. In such a phrase, "heaven" means simply *God*. Indeed, our confidence is in God, not in some heaven and certainly not in our own immortality. We die. But, for the New Testament, *eternal life* and the *risen life* begin now, here, in community with the assembly that bears witness to God's mercy in Christ. What such life will be hereafter we leave to God. And God is trustworthy. Still, one thing we do know, from the content and tenor of the Scriptures: whatever God's gift is in the face of death, it does not involve the abandoning of God's beloved and needy earth and all of its creatures in favor of a few human spirits getting out of here. The rainbow from Noah's story (Gen. 9:8-17) still rises over all the earth. The blood of Christ's cross still reconciles all things—*ta panta* (Col. 1:15-20)—to God.

But, in the gospel of Jesus Christ and in the life of the Christian assembly, that rainbow also rises over each person, in his or her own need and sorrow and loss. And that reconciliation also is given to each person as a beloved part of *ta panta*.

We die. It is good and appropriate to mourn any one of these deaths. According to the gospel tradition, Jesus does so himself (cf. John 11:33, 35). But the assembly around the gospel also draws us gently into trust in God in the face of death.

It belongs to the pastor to teach this biblical and liturgical conception of death in the current time. It also belongs to the pastor to hear this word herself or himself. It belongs to the pastor to be honest about the fact that he or she is mortal and to find in the gospel a daily renewal of hope and a daily end to fear, that endless source of bad decisions and selfish action.

Then, when we each actually come to die, it may be that the rehearsed honesty about death and the practiced habit of trust in God may help us. Patterns we learn through our lives do become patterns that also mark our deaths. Crabbed fear through life can become heightened fear at death. But, even at death itself, our trust is not in trust itself, but only in God. There we will need another to have the word of God and the prayers for us, others to hold and love and sing to us as this is possible, wise others to know when we need to be alone and when we need company—to know indeed that we are not dead yet! But we cannot promise ourselves a "good death." We may indeed be alone and afraid, struggling and angry. Honesty about this possibility is also important. Only God is our hope, not the excellence of our preparations for death.

But the honesty of the liturgy can indeed invite us to make such preparations. The pastor who speaks openly about death in the communal liturgy will find it personally wise to do what is possible to arrange property and financial affairs, make a will, be clear about medical measures that should or should not be taken, and think about his or her survivors, talking about all of these arrangements openly with them. In general, the pastor will find it wise not to hide from death— and not to be unhealthily obsessed with it either.

THE LITTLE DEATHS

Before this last death there will be the little deaths. They too invite us to trust in the life-giving God.

Pastors know a whole variety of little deaths. With everyone else they know of the moments of physical sickness or disability or the moments of letting go, of moving on, or of facing failure, all of which can be described in metaphoric language as having something of death about them. With every Christian, pastors also know the daily dying and rising that can come with hearing the word and promise of God or the mirror of death and resurrection that can be found in the cycle of sleeping and rising in every day. In each of these there is for Christians remarkable help in dealing with the little deaths.

But pastors specifically know their own kind of loss, as well. Accepting a new call or a new position can be an exhilarating undertaking, bringing with it a sense of new life. But it also may involve letting go an old form of life, commending a whole congregation to God and then letting them go. Pastors do wisely to separate themselves genuinely from old charges. But there is a little death in such letting go: *I cannot do it; it is not about me.* At the same time, a new position or a new call may need to be refused or it may be hoped for and then lost. Such transitions may be complicated even more by the unhappiness of the new or old position, by idealized memories or projections about either, and by the hopes or sadness or anger of the pastor's family amid transition. The change may thus become even more like actual dying, with all of its complex layers and diverse reactions, fears, and guilt. Here, too, the only hope is to trust in God who does indeed call us "to ventures of which we cannot see the ending, by paths as yet untrodden, through perils unknown." Courage for those ventures comes from God the life-giver, not from ourselves. Let the pastor weigh the voice of God in the current call or appointment and the voice of God in a new, beckoning call or appointment. Let the pastor listen seriously to his or her family and consult wise conversation partners. Let the pastor then freely choose, with courage, with joy in the vocation to serve an assembly as pastor, and with a clear sense that such a choice does not have to be perfect. God is the life-giver.

Vocational change for other people than pastors can also be complex, involving something of the little death. But, for pastors, the change is always mixed up with talk about God and God's call, sometimes in a way that is not very wise about the biblical God. Well, then, let the pastor remember that this God is full of mercy and forgiveness. One tries to make the right decision. Then, remembering Luther's striking advice to Philip Melanchthon, one does indeed sin boldly but trust and believe in Christ more boldly still. For pastors, there is no perfect place—no *just where I ought to be, just where God wants me to be.* Rather, every place is a good place for assembly, for preaching, for table serving, and for remembering the poor. Every place is a place to be loved and honored. Every place is a place for the strong center and the open door. Those engagements make up the vocation.

Such dynamics of the little death and the new beginning are involved also in other parts of a pastor's life. Retirement from full-time service may be one such occasion. It will be finally useful for pastors to know that they are not indispensable, that they have other things in their life than their assembly vocation, that they rightly let go and make room for others. But there may be something of death in this realization as well, and also pastors shy away from death. Let them not be afraid. God gives life.

Letting one's own children go may be another such occasion. Some parents let their children go easily, freely, delighting in these new adults. For others the transition is very hard, death-like. Pastors need to be especially wary here, since the children inevitably find God and church much involved with their parent's life. The necessary task of the child to leave home may come to have something in it of leaving church or God or both. For many pastors, this moment is difficult—and beyond their control. The child must be given over to God, let go.

In this regard, here is a proposal, a piece of countercultural counsel, an idea to weigh: it will probably be wise for pastors not to baptize or preside at the weddings of their own children. Similarly, it will be wise for pastors not to try to be their children's only pastor. It will be wise for pastors not to bury their own children, were their deaths to occur tragically before the pastor's own. Baptisms, weddings, and funerals already have a tendency in our cultures to be interpreted as simply family events, whereas, when these rites are held in church, they are intended to introduce their subjects into a wider family than their family of origin. In addition, while pastors can hardly desire to be as God in their own families, there is always the problem of the pastor being regarded as a stand-in for God. Of course, in some remote places, there may be nobody else to do the baptism or the burial or the wedding. Of course, many children will indeed receive the word of forgiveness in assembly and the bread of Holy Communion from their own parent. Still, it will be good for the pastor to occupy that role carefully, self-critically, looking for at least occasional relief. Remember Augustine: "Insofar as I am a bishop, I am in danger; insofar as I am a believer, I am safe." Ah, dear pastor, by all means, when you can, side by side with your children, be a struggling believer, hands out for mercy. Be in the congregation when your child is married and your grandchild baptized. Be side by side with your beloved ones, kneeling at the holy table. Do not know all the answers. On these occasions at least, for your sake but also for theirs, be safe. There may be a little death in this, but God is the life-giver—also for your children, also for your spouse, also for you.

But pastors, who are people who long to do good for other people, may especially face the little death in their own limits and inabilities. They cannot take away the sickness and the death that they encounter. They cannot solve a deep problem for another. They are welcomed to hear another's agony, to know another's painful situation, to hear a confession of sin, to enter into a long-hidden communal sorrow. But then they frequently must simply be there. They may help a little. The very fact that they listen may help relieve the awful loneliness of some burdens. But wise pastors nonetheless are frequently face-to-face with their own limits, their own helplessness in the face of sorrow, sin, and loss. They must simply keep silence and be there…*except* they *can* announce the forgiveness of sins. That is astonishing. It seems like such a little thing, but it can become the seed of life itself. More: Pastors can see that their own boundaried weakness is gathered into the very weakness of Christ. The wounded-risen Christ is there, side by side with the wounded other, the sinful other, the sorrowing others. The forgiveness of sins arises from this same Christ. So does the possibility of hope, even where the pastor honestly has nothing to give and can only give this other— these others—to God.

This boundaried weakness, this failure and inability, is also a little death. But, because of the life-giving God, it can also become the locus of a little resurrection.

Symbols of the Gospel

So, has this reflection on the life of the pastor, after all, become a law book? Does it all come down to this: Remember you are dying and be honest about it. And more: Study and pray. Keep the commandments. And more: Say the right words. Serve the table. Remember the poor. Is the spirituality of the pastor all about the things you must do?

No. Listen. At its deepest, the spirituality of the pastor is exactly about the things you cannot do. You come to the limits of your ability. You face the little deaths. You know from the words of the liturgy that you too will die. Luther rightly calls you—and himself and all pastors—dirt-bags, material for the worms. But the triune God—the God who holds the world in mercy, who joins all humanity in its need and death, who is poured out as the Spirit of hope—is the everlasting life-giver.

Listen. Dear pastor, this too is for you. Your baptism has joined you to Christ, gathered your death and your little deaths into his, raised you up with him and surrounded you with the mercy and the presence of this triune God. The Holy Supper feeds you with the bread of life and the cup of salvation. And the words of absolution—the "keys" given to Peter and to all of the Christians as they speak to one another—announce forgiveness to you. Let someone speak them to you.

We have come to that part of the catechism which is simply unmixed, over-whelming gift. You are involved daily—and at least weekly in the assembly—in giving that gift away. Now receive it yourself. There is nothing else to say.

Then your study and your prayer will simply be the Spirit holding you in that gift. Your daily life will be the discovery of surprises that may unfold in ordinary life when it is unfolded in the breath of that Spirit. And, more, your speaking the Word, your serving the table, your remembering the poor will flow freely from you as one who has learned the assembly-gift of the Spirit, the assembly-mercy of the triune God, by heart.

The spirituality of the pastor is this: life and death in that gift.

I have long found deep comfort in the words that Martin Luther wrote on a note found by his bedside when he himself was found dead in 1546. As recorded in the famous Table Talk, his deathbed note included this little assertion: "I say we are all beggars; this is true." Having learned about "growth in grace" and "sanctification" when I was a boy, studying my catechism, I often wondered if I was really making any progress. I thought probably not. But Luther helped me to see that growth in grace might really mean growth in need, growth in identification with a needy world and with other needy folk, growth in becoming more and more profoundly a beggar oneself, waiting upon God.

As a pastor, I need that word. The pastor's spirituality is finally a beggar's spirituality. "One beggar telling another beggar where there is bread," as the Tamil theologian D. T. Niles had it. The problem with the awful pastor in Ingmar Bergman's Winter Light *(in Swedish called* Nattvardsgæsterna *or "The Communicants"!) is that he is no beggar at all. He tries to be in control, tries to always help. But his transcendent god simply turns into a monster in the face of the actual need and death of the world and in the face of the unexplored need of his own soul.*

But here's the thing. There is bread.

In Gian Carlo Menotti's opera Amahl and the Night Visitors, *one of the Magi—seemingly nearly mad—carries around a portable box of personal treasures and candies. With Amahl himself as audience, he sings the wonderful song, "This is my box. This is my box. I never travel without my box!" When I was pastor in a university congregation that had no permanent meeting place, the various students who were setting up for the Sunday Eucharist and I used to carry several boxes across a street, across the campus and then into the space that we used for the assembly.*

I carried a box full of bread and chalices and liturgy books and vestments and, occasionally, a baptismal candle. Not uncommonly I would sing, "This is my box. This is my box. I never travel without my box!" The students often laughed and sang with me.

I think that pastors never travel without this box: Word and Sacraments full of the gospel of Jesus Christ for a needy assembly, for needy world. Bread. In fact, I think that there are no real pastors without this box. Maybe slightly mad, beggars all, carrying this box and bringing out its astonishing contents constitutes their spirituality.

WORKS CITED

Augustine. *On Christian Teaching*. Translated by R. P. H. Green. Oxford's World Classics. New York: Oxford University Press, 1997.

Babette's Feast. 1987. Written and directed by Gabriel Axel. DVD. Century City, Calif.: MGM Home Entertainment, 2001.

Bonhoeffer, Dietrich. *Life Together*. New York: Harper & Row, 1954.

Brilioth, Yngve. *A Brief History of Preaching*. Philadelphia: Fortress Press, 1965.

Brock, Sebastian, and Michael Vasey. *The Liturgical Portions of the* Didascalia. Bramcote: Grove, 1982.

Brother Roger. *Parable of Community*. London: Mowbray, 1980. (The quotation from the *Rule of Taizé* is from p. 13.)

Carter, Sydney. "I Come Like a Beggar." London: Stainer & Bell, Ltd., 1974, 1987.

Eusebius. *Ecclesiastical History*. vol. 1. Trans. Kirsopp Lake and J. E. L. Oulton. Loeb Classical Library 265. Cambridge: Harvard University Press, 1973, 1984.

Evangelical Lutheran Worship. Minneapolis: Augsburg Fortress, 2006. (The Prayer of the Day for Ash Wednesday, Eucharistic Prayer IV, and the prayer at the conclusion of Morning Prayer are quoted from this volume.)

Farella, John R. *The Main Stalk: A Synthesis of Navajo Philosophy*. Tucson: University of Arizona Press, 1990. (Quotation is from p. 16.)

Harlow, Rabbi Jules, ed. "Liturgy for Yom Kippur" from *Mahzor for Rosh Hashanah*. New York: The Rabbinical Assembly, 1972.

Herbert, George. *George Herbert: The Country Parson, The Temple*. Ed. John N. Wall Jr. New York: Paulist, 1981.

Hovda, Robert. *Strong, Loving, and Wise: Presiding in Liturgy*. Washington, D.C.: The Liturgical Conference, 1976.

Justin. *1 Apology*.

Kavanagh, Aidan. *Elements of Rite: A Handbook of Liturgical Style*. New York: Pueblo Publishing, 1982.

Lamott, Anne. *Traveling Mercies: Some Thoughts on Faith*. New York: Pantheon, 1999. (Quotation is from p. 82.)

Luther, Martin. "The Blessed Sacrament of the Holy and True Body of Christ, and the Brotherhoods." In *Luther's Works*, vol. 35: Word and Sacrament I. Trans. and ed. E. Theodore Bachmann. Philadelphia: Fortress Press, 1960. (Quotation is from p. 54.)

_____. "A Brief Instruction on What to Look for and Expect in the Gospels." In *Luther's Works*, vol. 35: Word and Sacrament I. Trans. and ed. E. Theodore Bachmann. Philadelphia: Fortress Press, 1960. (Quotation is from p. 121.)

_____. *A Contemporary Translation of Luther's Small Catechism*. Trans. Timothy Wengert. Minneapolis: Augsburg Fortress, 1996.

_____. *Table Talk. Luther's Works*, vol. 54. Trans. and ed. Theodore G. Tappert. Philadelphia: Fortress Press, 1967.

Lutheran World Federation. "Nairobi Statement on Worship and Culture." Geneva: Lutheran World Federation, 1996.

Menotti, Gian Carlo. *Amahl and the Night Visitors*. New York: G. Schirmer, 1986 (1951).

Plato. *Lysis Symposium Gorgias*. Trans. W. R. M. Lamb. Loeb Classical Library 166. Cambridge, Mass.: Harvard University Press, 1925.

Robinson, Marilynne. *Gilead: A Novel*. New York: Farrar, Straus and Giroux, 2004.

Steinbeck, John. *The Grapes of Wrath*. New York: Bantam, 1946 (1939). (Quotations are from pp. 16, 20.)

Tertullian. *Apology and De Spectaculis*. Trans. T. R. Glover. Loeb Classical Library 250. Cambridge, Mass.: Harvard University Press, 1977.

Winter Light. 1963. Written and directed by Ingmar Bergman. DVD. Criterion Collection, 2003.

Williams, Rowan. *Christian Spirituality: A Theological History from the New Testament to Luther and St. John of the Cross*. Atlanta: John Knox, 1979.

INDEX